Helen and Bob Fischer, Ro̶̶ ̶ ̶ ̶ ̶ ̶ ̶ ̶ ̶ ̶i̶s̶c̶h̶e̶r̶, Ali & David Jones, Rian & David Burchfiel, Suzanne Newbrough Diaz, Richard & Liz Melton, Candace Price, Christina Powell, Ann Huffsmith, Port Moore, Rick Corns, Liat & David Zilberman, Red & Aquina Anderson, Ashley Wren Collins, Francisco Roldan, Rhonda Coullet, Marshall Albritton, Mary & Van Hedges, June Houghton Kingsbury, Milt Capps, Anne & Tom Occhipinti, Tim Albaugh, Ben Gotlieb, Hugh Sinclair, McCarty Baker, Matthew Napoli, Bowen & Victoria Stovall, Laura James, New York University, Lipscomb University, Melissa Forte, Theatre East, Aurora Theatre, Tennessee Playwrights Studio, Pipeline-Collective Salon, Dramatists Guild, ProPath Screenwriting, Dr. Monica Stout, Dr. Kevin Rankin, Dr. Brett Parker, Dr. Hardin, Dr. Christian Rhea, Dr. Spalding Green and the many other people, doctors and nurses who have helped us along the way.

TABLE OF CONTENTS

Disclaimer

I am not a doctor, nurse or medical professional nor am I here to provide medical help. All of the medications, procedures, helpful hints and opinions listed in this book are just that, opinions that are based on the health and well-being of two very particular people, my parents. Please check with medical professionals re: what would be best for you or someone you are caretaking before using any products, taking any medications or taking the advice mentioned in this book. I, the author, hereby disclaim any and all responsibility for any liability, loss or risk re: choices made based on the tips and stories found in the contents of this book.

PROLOGUE

. . . .

This book is a "self-help-how-to-memoir." Based on my personal experiences as a caregiver, the book is chock full of the many tips and coping mechanisms that I've learned along the way. After five years of caregiving and counting, I've decided to put the bits of wisdom that I've gained re: my parents into this book with the hope that some of what I've learned/experienced might be an encouragement to others embarking on their own caregiving journey. It's also a chance for me to mark the miles I've come thus far. The book is for anyone who's looking for insight into elder care, anyone who is contemplating taking the task of caregiving on, and those who love me and are interested in the paths I've tread. I'm not a doctor, surgeon or nurse. So, my thoughts re: various procedures, medications, ways of helping are just that, my thoughts, garnered from my experiences with two very specific people, my parents.

Taking care of them has been a trip, both internally and externally. I am definitely not the same person I was five years ago and neither are they. And physically, well, all of us (mom, dad, me, you) are getting older with every breath that we breathe. And that journey, the journey of aging, of growing as we age, is also a topic I'd like to address.

I believe we find a fuller version of ourselves in service towards others. And yet, we live in a world where everyone (myself included) operates in a big self-absorbed circle. We look for validation on social media and we post photos that depict ourselves always happy and successful. I often feel a sense of emptiness after scrolling on my socials. I feel less connected, not more. I feel less empathetic after an hour of scrolling, not more. Service, however, actually showing up in the trenches of another's hardship, brings out, in my opinion, more of who we are meant to be. It demands that we be fully present and connected. Growing old is a gift. But growing old, the gradual breakdown of the body is often marked with major setbacks and hardships. We live in a youth absorbed society. What I mean is, we are collectively petrified of growing old. And so, our wise elders are often ushered away and out of sight with limited visitations. Why do we do this? Are our lives more important than helping those who helped us first? I'm not meaning to guilt trip. For, I do believe that sometimes the load is too much to bear for one person or even two. Full blown dementia/Alzheimer's involves 24/7 care as do other all-encompassing illnesses. And some conditions simply require daily contact with a medical staff. But still, for the most part, I think we as a society tuck folks away too often and too soon.

There is much to be gained by pouring ourselves out: kindness, patience, empathy, deep friendship and the beauty of helping another human make their way through, what can be, quite frightening terrain. We also potentially gain a part of ourselves that we can only find when easing the anxiety and pain of others.

Should I care less or care more?

1

. . . .

After a few years of praying, "Should I move back to Nashville?" And way too frequent flights for my actor/ writer/adjunct professor budget, I decided to move from New York City to Tennessee. Let me be 1000% clear, I absolutely love New York City. It is the place I consider home. I love the theater scene, which is why I moved there. I love my fabulously talented, full-of-heart friends. I love the diversity of people. I love the food, the museums, the list goes on and on. So, leaving New York was not an easy decision. Thus, the praying for numerous years before heading south. I just didn't like the idea of leaving the best (in my opinion) city in the world. But our mom had been diagnosed with Parkinson's and, although she wasn't in dire straights, I was traveling back and forth at least once a month, which was simply not tenable. I needed to either care less or… care more.

Let me back track a bit. I had lived in NYC for almost thirty-two years. So, my roots were quite deep. I was (and still am) an adjunct professor at New York University where I've been teaching my Writing Great Characters course since 2010, as well as casting actors for the NYU Steinberg (now called Rehearsal Process) class since 2009. I was also a teaching artist from 2009-2019 in the NYC public after school system. (Teaching fourth and fifth graders acting and playwriting was one of my favorite freelance gigs.)

I moved to New York to pursue acting. (As an actress I've appeared in commercials, films, regional theater and Off-Broadway.) And somewhere along the way, I fell in love with writing as well. I am a published playwright, produced screenwriter and recorded songwriter. One of my favorite songwriting gigs was getting hired by Sony Wonder/ Golden Books to write a kids album/video based on the book *Pat the Bunny*. The end product was *Pat the Bunny Sing with* Me, a ten song album based on the aforementioned book. As you can see, I wore/wear many hats. Being around other artists was, and continues to be, profoundly inspiring and impactful. While in NYC, I often acted with and was produced by Theatre East. This group of consummate actors/directors/artists brought me more joy than I can express by casting me in their beautiful productions and by producing two of my short plays and my full-length play *Petie*. My play *Petie* was the reason I had gone to grad school. I had written a short story titled *Petie* and, when I would read the story out loud, I had the sense that the piece was meant to be a full-length play. The problem was I had no idea how to turn it into one. So, I applied to New York University's MFA Program to figure it out. And thanks to the brilliant playwright Eduardo Machado, who helped me free my core writing voice and my writing professor Daniel Goldfarb, my play *Petie* was born. Shout out to Starving Artists in North Carolina who produced the first production of *Petie* as well. In fact, God bless all theaters that produce first productions. It takes such heart and courage to produce a show first or even second knowing that the play will undergo massive rewrites during the course of that first production process. And while I'm at it, thanks Adirondack Theatre Festival for producing my musical *Barbara's Blue Kitchen* and Capitol Rep. for being the first to produce my and Don Chaffer's musical *The Sparkley Clean Funeral Singers*! https://www.concordtheatricals.com/p/59980/the-sparkley-clean-funeral-singers

I mention my writing history to give you context re: who I am and to delve into some of the artistic adventures I've thus far had. Secondly, to show the deep feelings about and deep roots I had grown into the ground of New York. But here's the thing, I love NYC, but I love my parents more. They regularly inspire and delight me and I genuinely like being in their presence. So, in the summer of 2019, I began deciding what to keep and what to throw away. I did the math re: a moving truck. I looked at all of my furniture and asked myself, "What am I absolutely attached to?" My answer was my writing desk and a flowered wingback chair. Everything else felt disposable. And in the end, I didn't even keep the desk or chair. In fact, I moved via the U.S. Postal Service. I shipped box after box of clothing, books, oh, so many books, papers, lamps, art, silverware, I shipped it all. And minus five hundred dollars later, I found myself and my cat Edna back in the great state of Tennessee.

Did I miss the big apple? Yes, daily. But after all that time praying, I felt peace about being back in Music City. Did I mention that our dad is a songwriter? (Dad co-wrote the Reba song *You Lie*, along with Austin Roberts and Charlie Black.) We were originally from the midwest. Our dad grew up poor in Iowa with a dream of being a songwriter and our mom grew up middle class in Illinois with a dream of staying in Illinois, close to family. Mom's absolute love for her mom most definitely influenced my move back to Tennessee. Growing up, our family vacations consisted of mom piling me and my brother into the car to head back to Illinois where my grandmother lived. No long beach trips, no mountains, no exotic views, just family. And, since I'd never been on an exotic vacation, I didn't really know to miss fancy vacations because **family** vacations were all that I (and my brother Robbi) knew. We did have one beach trip as children. Dad drove us to Florida. We sat on the beach staring at the ocean for the better part of an hour. Then, he piled us back into the car and we headed home. I literally still had sand on my butt. When asked about that trip later in life. Dad simply said, "I just wanted to show you the ocean." (I think my parents were also struggling financially and possibly didn't have money for a hotel.) Back to the story at hand, our mom agreed to move to Nashville to support our dad's dream, but her heart was always torn between family in Illinois and our family in Tennessee. So, that will affect you or at least it affected me. And, if you have to move back to a city, Nashville is a beautiful place to be. **Takeaway: When faced with a choice to care more or less, choose to care more.**

Compression Fracture

2

. . . .

The first harrowing experience occurred in what I thought was the least likely place, the gym. Let me first say, our mom has gone to the gym going on thirty years. She wasn't a big weight lifter, yoga guru or cyclist, but she thoroughly enjoyed water aerobics. She went three times a week and had made numerous lasting friendships over the many years she put on her bathing suit and plunged into the pool. After my move to Nashville, we had the perfect gym routine. She'd trot off towards the locker room/pool. I'd trot off to lift weights and/or ride the stationary bike. Me listening to a podcast. Mom chatting with her friends as they splashed in the water. All was good until the day the pool was closed for a swim meet and the instructor brought the seniors into the weight room. Let me say this clearly. **DO NOT BRING A BUNCH OF SENIORS WHO MIGHT HAVE OSTEOPOROSIS TO THE WEIGHT ROOM**

UNLESS YOU ARE TRAINED RE: HOW TO HELP SENIOR CITIZENS LIFT WEIGHTS IN A HEALTHY, NON-HARMFUL MANNER.

From the upstairs track, I saw a group of seniors gathered around our mom. So, I headed downstairs. Evidently, mom had just tried out the standing calf shoulder press. The way this machine works is the weight is on your shoulders and you rise up and down, which strengthens the calf muscles. I've done this many times over the years. But the thing is, mom has severe osteoporosis. She rose up, heard a pop and felt pain. To say the least, I was alarmed and the opposite of happy with the water aerobics instructor. How dare she encourage our mom, who knew next to nothing about weight lifting, to work out on a standing calf shoulder press? How dare she set my trusting, elderly fragile-boned mom, to doing of all things this machine? Wanting to stay focused on mom's pain rather than my anger towards the aforementioned water aerobics instructor, I assessed the situation, got mom out of there and off we went to TOA, the Tennessee Orthopedic Alliance, where they x-rayed mom's back and diagnosed her with a **compression fracture.**

Mom was prescribed rest and pain meds. However, she found getting in and out of bed, even with pain medication, extremely difficult. My friend Laura had given me her mother's back wedge pillow after her mom, my godmother Belle had passed away. The **back wedge/bed wedge pillow** is a wedged pillow that allows the injured person to sleep on an angle. So, getting up and down isn't

13

as traumatic. To see mom in so much pain was a heartbreak, but thankfully, the pillow, rest and meds helped. And, after eight long weeks, mom was back to her normal self. In fact, once she recovered, mom was back at the gym doing water aerobics. The tricky part for me was that the same negligent instructor was still working there, but mom wanted to go so... Thankfully, the negligent instructor, unrelated to us, unexpectedly left and a new instructor, appeared on the scene. And, as per mom's request, we went back to our routine of mom doing her water aerobics while I lifted weights and/or rode the stationary bike. **Takeaway: If your loved one has osteoporosis, but wants to lift weights, consult with a trained professional. Doing weight bearing activity can be a wonderful workout addition when done properly.**

Go to the Dermatologist

3

. . . .

I regularly go to the dermatologist. So, after moving to Nashville, I decided to schedule my parents for a dermatological check up and boy am I glad that I did.

Because Dr. Hardin, our dermatologist found and removed a patch of squamous skin carcinoma (the second most common type of skin cancer according to Google) on dad's back. When caught early, this type of skin cancer is curable, but left unchecked, larger SCC's can be harder to treat and fast growing. (Yikes.) **Takeaway: No matter how old your loved one is, take them to the dermatologist and take yourself there too while you're at it.**

Heart Attack

4

The past few days had been glorious in every way. My short film *i only miss you when i'm breathing* (https://www.ionlymissyouwhenimbreathing.com/) had just debuted at the Nashville Film Festival. My friend, the director, Ashley Wren Collins, had flown in for the premiere. The amazing cast attended along with many wonderful friends who made time to see our labor of love. Joy was ringing in the rafters. There's so much that goes into making a short film and the competition for each and every film festival is fierce. So, to get chosen by the

Nashville Film Festival and to get to see our film on the big screen was thrilling. The film, which deals with grief, was written as a tribute to our dear friends Freddy and Pippy Weller who had lost their son Brandon years before. After the final screening, I continued the celebration with a friend outside in my gazebo. It was the evening of October 9th, 2019 and, as we toasted to success, my cup was literally running over. Until…

The next morning when dad said he didn't feel well. I'm asking him questions, trying to suss out his symptoms when he says "I think I should go to the emergency room." Mom, Dad and I pile into the car and head over to the St. Thomas Midtown ER. Just the fact that dad wants to go to the hospital is alarming. He's simply not "that guy." He's the take an extra Tylenol and move on guy. I can still see the three of us waiting in that waiting room. After hanging around for a while, dad seemed okay and he expressed an interest in leaving. As we got up to go though, they called dad's name, took him into a room and took some tests. After looking at the test results, however, they couldn't say what was wrong with him, but they did suggest that he stay for observation. Dad said, "No, I want to go home." So, home we went. We ate lunch. Mom and Dad napped. I graded homework in the aforementioned gazebo. (I teach screenwriting classes at Lipscomb University in addition to my teaching job at New York University.) So, there I was sitting in the exact spot where I had celebrated the night before when mom came into the gazebo and said, "I think we need to go back to the hospital." With dread, I went into the house. "Where's dad?" I asked. Mom said, "He's already outside waiting to go." I looked out the window and there he was, leaning on the car. I can't explain how I knew what I knew. When you know someone your whole life, you just know things and I knew by the way he was leaning on the car that dad was dying.

To tell this next part, I have to give a little personal history/context. As I've mentioned, I lived in NYC for just shy of 32 years. And for some reason, I often thought, "What would I do in case of an emergency? Given how backed up traffic in New York City can be, would I call an ambulance or would I hail a cab? And I had decided that, unless bleeding profusely, I would hail a cab. Well, one day as I walked to work a cabaret show at Don't Tell Mama's Piano Bar and Cabaret Club, Soli, this amazing, kind soul, who also happens to be the cleaning woman at DTM, flagged me down as I approached. She said, "Bobby," the lighting designer for the cabaret club, "thinks he is having a heart attack" and that "he had been waiting for me to arrive." I took one look at Bobby and hailed the nearest taxi. It was smooth sailing until we got to West 59th Street and Central Park South. Suddenly, the cab seemed to veer towards the right. "What are you doing?" I shouted. The cab driver pointed to a white stretch limo on his left and said, "That guy won't let me in." "Don't you dare turn right." I said. To turn right would set us on a course towards a hospital on the upper east side and would add a good twenty to thirty minutes to our ride. Whereas, the hospital I was aiming to get us to was, at that point, a literal, three

17

minute drive away. I lunged half of my torso out of the window and screamed at the limo driver, "This man is having a heart attack, let us over!" Because his window was down (it was a beautiful day) the man heard my screech and let our cab merge into his lane. We pulled up to the hospital, I escorted Bobby in and then, I hopped in another cab and headed back downtown towards West 46th Street for the aforementioned cabaret show. And let me just say, when the cab turned left to drive down 9th Avenue it was wall-to-wall traffic. Had I called an ambulance, we would have still been waiting for the paramedics to arrive. (Whereas, the taxi had gotten Bobby to the hospital in ten minutes.) I hopped out of the cab and walked the rest of the way back to the club.

After the show, I went back to the hospital to check in on Bobby. As I entered his room, he said, "The cardiologist told me to tell you that you saved my life by getting me to the hospital so fast."

Let me be clear here, of course a person should call an ambulance because the paramedics will give lifesaving care as soon as they arrive. However, when I looked at dad, I knew that we were down to mere minutes and it was pre-pandemic Nashville traffic, which meant, it would most likely take around twenty minutes for the ambulance to get to us. So, I did the math and opted to drive. Mom was trying to put on her shoes. I said, "No time for shoes, put them on in the car." I got dad in and off we went.

There I was trying to turn right/reliving, almost to the letter, my New York experience because the car to my left wasn't gonna let me in. So, I, once again, leaned out the window and yelled, "Let me in, my dad's having a heart attack." The driver waved my car in, the light changed and off I sped. While driving, dad asked that I call my brother. He wanted to hear his son's voice in case this was it. My brother is a minister and as I drove, he prayed and the prayer was so comforting to dad as our car roared towards the hospital. Seven minutes later, I pulled up to the emergency room. At that point dad said, he couldn't get himself out of the car. So I did the thing I've seen in so many movies. I ran into the ER, yelling, "My dad's having a heart attack." Suddenly, a gurney with nurses attached appeared. As they got dad out of the car, one of the nurses hurriedly told me to take my car to valet parking. Then, they whisked dad away with mom trailing along after them.

Wait. **The ER has valet parking**? I drove the thirty feet to what I hoped was valet parking and tossed the keys to a nearby man. As I bolted into the hospital, I had this thought, "What if I just gave the car keys to someone not associated with the hospital?" No time to check, there I was asking where they'd taken dad and hurrying to mom's side. As I entered the ER room, I found dad legitimately in the throes of death. He looked cold, clammy and pale as a sheet. In direct opposition to the upheaval that was going on in dad's body, a calm voice to our right was telling us that the on-call team was en route and would be here shortly and that, as soon as the on-call team arrived, they would take dad to the already prepped operating room. The minutes were passing, dad was passing and then, there they were, wheeling dad away and ushering mom and I to a nearby waiting room. This whole process: helping dad into the car, speeding through traffic, getting him into the ER, me throwing the car keys to the valet, then, witnessing dad in the throes of death, the on-call team arriving took a total of fifteen minutes. And in that time, the three of us were changed forever.

Once in the waiting room, mom and I prayed. We prayed for the excellence of the surgeon and the entire on-call team, prayed for dad's resilience, prayed for dad's healing. I texted my prayer partners, I updated my brother, I called dad's sisters. Oddly enough, this part gets tricky. But it does bring up a good, hard point. Sometimes when you're in crisis, the very people who can hurt you the most are family. I thought about not including this part in the book, but my reason for writing the book is to help other caregivers. So, here goes. (Don't worry, it's not that big of a hurt, but it is worth unpacking.) I called dad's siblings so that they could be praying for him. They expressed gratitude that I had called and kept them in the loop. Within minutes, however, another family member texted a reprimand forbidding me from sharing bad news with their mom/my aunt. Let me be clear, I had no idea calling was "off limits." And I have no problem with their wanting to protect someone from upsetting news. But I'd already made the call, I'd already broken the rule that I didn't know existed and I'm sitting in the waiting room, waiting to hear if my dad lives or dies. Now is not the time for the reprimand. The reprimand was ill-timed and beyond upsetting. Thankfully, I had my head on straight and I knew that I had to immediately detach from the text. **I had to stay focused on praying for dad and being present with mom. So, that's what I did.** I'm sharing this story because these kinds of things often occur in families. You're in the trenches, at the hospital, begging God to let your loved one live and someone, someone you love, someone who loves you, cuts you down. Again, to have a conversation with me about the boundaries they were pursuing for their mother would have been more than fine after some time had passed, but to scold me while dad was splayed out on the OR table was jarring. Looking back, I know and I knew even then, they were simply protecting their mom. People, all people are broken and sometimes our breaks cut each other. And all I could say, over and over to myself at the time was, "Lord, please give the cardiologist skillful, steady hands. Please give dad's heart resilience and healing." Again, that family member isn't a bad person. They are, in fact, an extremely good and loving person. But their timing did not take in that I myself had just been through an extremely harrowing event. What can I say? These are the things that happen in families. But I don't think we should write people off when they make mistakes. I definitely don't want to be written off when I make mistakes. The best course of action, in my humble opinion, is to stay focused on what is most important and then later try and see things from their point of view and, if it feels like it will be helpful, try to communicate how the experience felt for you at that time with the hope of deeper understanding on both sides.

I did at long last, broach this subject with my dear cousin. It was good to share my perspective and equally good to hear her side of the story. She told me that her mom was alone at the time of my call and that she, my cousin, feared, had things taken a drastic downturn, that I might call her mother back with even worse news re: her baby brother/ my dad. It's so insightful to hear the other person's perspective. Isn't it? We often don't keep the channel open for fear that our feelings won't be validated or heard, but I think, when possible, it's best to reach out and try to connect. And I am so glad that I did because the conversation with my cousin was wonderful. So much so, she gave me her blessing re: including the story in this book! Life is short and **love is allowed to say ouch.** The key reason for bringing this part of the story up is to acknowledge how tricky family dynamics can become. **My advice is, don't get sidetracked by family drama, keep your focus on what is most important, which is tenderly, expertly caretaking the person or persons in your charge.**

Back to the story at hand, after a relatively short amount of time, we were told that dad had made it through the procedure alive and well. We were escorted to his room. And boy howdy were we glad to see him. He had on an oxygen mask and he was hooked up to all sorts of tubes and beeping machines, but he was surprisingly alert. To say we were relieved is putting it lightly. We gave out hugs, expressed hallelujahs and, because we were all exhausted, hunkered down for the night. Mom lounged in an easy chair and I set up camp on the very cold floor behind dad's bed. (Big thanks to our friend Marshall who brought us extra blankets.)

Around four a.m., mom, who hadn't slept at all, and I left to grab a quick nap and a change of clothes at home. At seven a.m., we headed back to the hospital to find an outright chipper Bobby Fischer. Giddy to see us, he recounted his experience of the heart attack. After I'd rushed into the hospital looking for help, dad, feeling like this might be "the end" for him, turned to our mom and said, "It's been good."

After an hour or so, Dad's cardiologist, Dr. Kevin Rankin, came into the room and told us that dad's artery had been 99% blocked. He also praised me for getting dad to the hospital so fast. Saying, "If dad hadn't gotten to the hospital so quickly, he would have died." This information was helpful to me because I knew/know that 99% of the time calling for an ambulance is clearly the better choice, but to quote Joe Lewis, "I was doing the best I could with what I had at the time." (Also, no matter what happens in my life, I have the good feeling of knowing that I've helped two people, both named Bobby, survive heart attacks.) Still, my overall recommendation is that you **call an ambulance in times of emergency.**

One important thing to remember: **If you have a loved one in the hospital, make sure they stay hydrated.** The nurses had a terrible time getting blood samples from dad while he was there. In fact, one of the nurses poked him so much and so hard dad said it "almost felt worse than the heart attack." Why was getting a blood sample so difficult? Later, a different, quite wonderful nurse came in and mentioned that dad might be dehydrated and that he needed to drink more water. I immediately got dad on the "drinking water case" and, sure enough, the next time a nurse came in to get a blood sample it was easy peasy.

By day two of dad's two and a half day stint in the hospital, my brother Robbi and sister-in-law Janet arrived. And my brother, thankfully, stayed with dad that second night. After which, we brought dad home. They had put two stents into his heart by way of his wrist. The incision was so small, you can't even see a scar anymore. Modern science is amazing. Let me say that again, they put two stents into dad's heart by way of his wrist! How is that even possible? To say the least, we were all praising God.

Our dad truly is quite wonderful. He loves to write country songs and tell jokes. In fact, here's an example: At Dad's first appointment with Dr. Rankin post heart attack/ post hospitalization, the doctor entered looking at dad's info and without missing a beat dad said, "Are you doctor rank and file?" Dr. Rankin, caught off guard, let out a belly laugh. Then, dad pointed to his socks, which have photos of our mom on them and said, "Have you met my wife?" Another laugh. If he were to meet you, dad's sole goal would be to tell you a joke, a story or play you one of his songs. Pretty uplifting life goals. I would say.

Two weeks after dad's heart attack, they had him signed up for cardiac rehab. And let me say, it was tricky finding the place. **Always allow extra time, especially if going to**

an appointment at a hospital. Hospitals can be quite sprawling/difficult to navigate and hurrying through hallways can be stressful. Doubly stressful if you're hurrying around with someone who's just had a heart attack. Not wanting to make mom walk too much, not wanting dad to walk too fast/get out of breath as we searched and searched for the exercise room was an experience, but we got there. And let me tell you, it was quite the thing, watching dad ride a bike so soon after the heart attack, but he's such a people person, he took to it like a duck to water. So much so, he drove himself to the subsequent appointments and wasted no time connecting with his fellow heart attack survivors. Rehab not only helped dad, it also set him on a course of regular exercise because after he graduated from rehab, he started, for the first time, going to the gym with mom on a regular basis.

Eleven days after dad's heart attack, I found my cat Edna lying in a place she had never been. The sweet girl was tucked away behind a box behind a tub. I knew something was wrong. Cats often hide when they don't feel well. I took her to the vet where I learned that Edna had kidney disease, a heart murmur and hyperthyroidism. When it rains it pours. I loved that cat so much. In fact, I had named her after my dear aunt Edna. And to find out this tragic news just after going through such a harrowing time with dad, well, it was a heartbreak. I held that sweet creature so close, thanking her for being such a good friend over the years. And then, taking the veterinarian's advice and not wanting her to be in any more pain, I let her go. **Takeaway:**

Call an ambulance when your loved one is having a heart attack. Stay hydrated, stay focused on what's important and, if an ER doctor recommends that you stay for observation, stay for observation.

Thank God for Lifeguards

5

Here's another gym experience. One day as I pumped a bit of iron in the weight room, a frantic trainer ran up to me saying my mother needed me at the pool. I ran at breakneck speed to reach mom, who was curled up on the concrete. In the water aerobics class, the seniors often held floaties out in front of them as they kicked their legs. Well, **mom had fallen forward over her floatie and was unable to pull herself back up**. I am sure that this happened because her back had been weakened by the compression fracture. Anyway, a lifeguard had jumped in and saved her from drowning. Side note: mom has always been very particular about her hair. Even as she did water aerobics, she always somehow managed to keep her hair dry. So, to see her lying poolside with her head completely

26

wet was jarring. From then on, I started taking the water aerobics class with mom.

I didn't give up weight lifting. For that, I scheduled other times to work out on my own at the gym. **I mention this to point out that self-care must be maintained while caregiving.** Eating healthy, taking walks, getting enough sleep is simply a must. caregiving requires every part of yourself. Psychologically, you will be tested, especially if the person you're taking care of is the person who raised you. **No matter how good your childhood was, you will, at times, be triggered, impatient, hurt. If you let it, caregiving can put you on a road to self-healing. It can burn away the dross and turn you into gold. It can make you more patient, more loving, more clear. But, it is my belief, if you don't take care to take care of yourself, you will burn out fast, possibly get sick yourself and become bitter and/or angry**. How do I know? Because I've, at times, been all of the above. As the person you're taking care of ages, they become laser focused on the things they want and, over time, become less of the parent you once knew. This can be difficult. There you are pouring yourself out like water and your loved one is oftentimes forgetting to say a simple "thank you." This can be painful. I guess it depends on what you're looking for in life, who you want to be. My personal goal is to become the kindest version of myself as I age. So that, on the day I die, I am the wisest, most loving version of myself. Will this be the case? Who knows? It's a goal. I have no idea if I'll get there. It sounds noble, yes, but I'm still human, which is code for broken. What I do know is that I have no chance of giving from a good place if my own tank is empty. **Sleep, healthy food, exercise, vacations and friends are of utmost importance.** I'm also a big believer in prayer. So, praying with my various prayer partners has helped me through many a hard day. I also continue to work on my art and go to artistic events as often as possible. Art is definitely my self-love love language. In fact, the very week mom had the epic pool event, I travelled to Rome, Georgia for a screening of my short film *i only miss you when i'm breathing* at the Rome International Film Festival. I felt trepidation regarding going because it felt a bit soon to be leaving her, but dad reassured me that all would be well. So, off I went.

   As caregivers, it's important that we do things that nourish us/fill our cups. And, after such a stressful week, the film festival was an absolute delight. I drove to Georgia with Pippy Weller. Once there, we ate great food, met awesome people, like Douglas and Dianemarie Collins with Alzheimer's Centers of America, and we got to see, along with director Ashley Wren Collins, our film on yet another big screen. Afterwards, there was a talkback and one woman (a grieving mother) told us that our film completely captured what she had been going through. I was glad that I went and equally happy was the time spent driving with Pippy. **Takeaway: Even when caregiving, find ways to enrich your own life and heart. Don't give up every part of yourself. Doing so will drain you and leave you an empty shell. Seek out ways to keep your**

own soul nurtured and you'll have more to give because your resource hasn't run dry.

Covid

6

As soon as Covid came on the scene, I knew that "something evil this way was coming." How did I know? My gut told me. I looked online and saw that there were, at that point, eleven reported cases. I can't say how I knew. I just knew that we were on the verge of something truly bad. Why tell this part of the story? Well, I want to encourage you to **trust your gut** whether it's about a deadly virus or a feeling that you might have left the stove on. (Turn the car around and go check the oven.) I learned to trust my gut early on in NYC. I'd been in town a year or so and on a grey November day, I turned west on W 54th Street and saw a tall, slender man walking east. My instinct said, "Cross the street." But because the man was wearing a suit, I ignored my gut. As I neared, the guy lunged towards me. The good news is, I was a runner and was able to quickly bolt away, evading whatever harm he intended, but lesson learned.

29

From then on, I trusted that inner voice. If I felt a sudden fight or flight jolt, I immediately crossed the street no questions asked. I didn't question my gut, I just removed myself from the situation and I want to encourage you to trust your gut as well.

Anyway, back to the coronavirus. Sure enough, the numbers continued to quickly rise and on March 15th, 2020, as I'm sure you know, the world suddenly shut down. What a strange time, Covid was. For the rest of 2020, I ordered our groceries online. In fact, everything went online. Suddenly, my classes, communicating with friends, meetings, all were online.

Mom, dad and I fell into a rhythm. We ate healthy food, played cards and watched a string of old movies. Dad and Mom both turned eighty-five that year. And when family members drove in to celebrate, we celebrated outside under the carport or spread out on the deck. For Christmas, we zoomed our holiday greetings. Dad, and this is a big thing, didn't go to the horse track during that hardcore Covid time. Dad has gone to the race track to bet on the horses every Saturday for years, but he didn't go. Instead, he bet online. He didn't want to bring the virus back to mom. Such love between those two!

As I write this, I realize that after Covid, mom has never been left alone. A shift occurred during 2020 and at some point during that year, mom no longer felt comfortable being left alone. This was a shock to me because mom had always been such a trailblazer. Just brave. Not loud, not needing attention, but so lovely and lively at every turn. So loving. So clear. When dad moved to Nashville for two years to see if he could make it as a songwriter, she got a job and single-handedly supported my brother and I. (Side note, for the two years dad lived in TN without us, he made the trek home every month to see us/make sure all was well on the home front.) And then, when dad moved the family to TN, mom found a job and new friends, no problem. And later, when she decided in her late 40s to become a nurse, she enrolled in college, studied hard and became an RN. So, for mom to suddenly be fearful of being alone, well, that was a blow. But life is about change and if she feels uncomfortable being alone, dad and I are more than willing to surround her with love.

Something that vastly improved my Covid experience was regularly meeting with friends over zoom. We called it our Friday happy hour. Drinking wasn't required, but camaraderie was. The group stemmed from the folks I knew from Theatre East, a group of fellow actors, directors, writers etc. Meeting with them really grounded each week. Having a place to land where I felt seen and accepted was a lifeline during that singular, strange year. Even now, as I recall the many nights we spent together over zoom, I long to see each and every one of them.

Having people who care about you as you care for others makes such a difference. Caregiving can be lonely at times. Pouring yourself out like water, sometimes you wonder, what about me? Who's pouring metaphorical water into me? And many times, the answer is no one. Caregivers are a rare breed. Many people are just not equipped to stay in the trenches of caregiving day after day. Add in how busy everyone is, most people are simply too wrapped up in their own life to wonder if someone else might be overtaxed with all the cooking, shopping, cleaning, bathing, pill dispensing, entertaining and driving back and forth for all of the doctor visits. This realization is a hard one. The question is, what do you do in these lonely moments? Well, first off, **taking other people's behavior personally is a waste of time**. People are gonna do or not do what they're gonna do or not do. Also, what they choose to do/how they respond or ignore is about them and how you choose to react is about you. How I choose to react is about me.

One thing that I started doing in 2019, that also helped me through the 2020 pandemic and continues to help me even now is listening to Libby, the library app. In fact, I have listened to over 320 books since April 2019. I listen while I garden, while I cook, while I walk. And that time, that time spent in the imaginary world of the various authors has been a lifeboat. The social justice books give me new perspectives, the fiction gives me delight, the memoirs give me insight, and the biographies and history books give knowledge. There's something great about being taken to a completely different place for a while, away from any personal concerns and into the wondrous world of a book. During Covid, books allowed me to see beyond the limited world we were all being forced to live in. Books gave me hope about a future after Covid. **Takeaway: Trust**

your gut, surround yourself with people who care about you and read or listen to more books.

Constipation and a Broken Arm

7

· ·

As the year wore on, I noticed that mom's balance had become increasingly uncertain. With that in mind, I had been asking her (repeatedly) to wait for me before getting out of the car. Our driveway is on a slant with a two foot drop on the side. We had just returned from running errands. We pulled into the driveway and as I turned the car around, I felt one of the tires run over something. There is a stray grey cat, that we call "Grey Boy" that often comes around the house and just to make sure nothing bad had happened, I put the car in park and looked under the car. It was just a stick. I had run over a stick. Well, during the brief span of time that I had put the car in park and checked to see what was under the tire, mom had gotten out of the car. I got back in the car and as I looked forward, I saw dad coming out the back door to greet us. Then, dad broke into a run. I knew without even looking that mom was falling.

She had lost her footing and was currently barreling towards that two foot precipice. I jumped out of the car and to my horror, there she was lying in a clump on the side of the driveway. She had a terrible gash on her wrist and her arm was in extreme pain. Thankfully, I had had the wherewithal to bring a wheelchair home after my godmother Belle had passed away for a "just in case" moment such as this. After sussing out if mom's leg or hip was broken, which they weren't, I told dad not to move her and asked mom not to move. Then, I raced inside and got the wheelchair. We carefully got mom up and into the wheelchair and then, wheeled mom inside where I called TOA for advice. (Tennessee Orthopedic Alliance has an emergency clinic.) I described mom's condition and, since mom wasn't in a life threatening situation, they told us to drive her to the TOA emergency clinic. Once there, they set mom's arm, **wrapped her injured wrist in a derma band (to seal the wound**) and sent us home with instructions and a prescription for pain pills. The arm was broken high up on her arm, almost to the shoulder. It was awful. Every stinking bit of this part of the caregiving journey was just awful. To see our sweet mom in so much pain, not to mention the hideous gash on her wrist, was heart sinking. A few days later, we took mom back to TOA where they did a CT scan of her abdomen and chest. She had been experiencing a stomach ache and they wanted to rule out any internal damage. After the scan, they informed us that there were no other fractures, no organ damage and no inflammation.

After several days on the pain meds, mom was completely constipated and to my immense chagrin, I had to give her a suppository and ultimately a fleet enema. The opposite of fun. Also, nerve wracking. I was very concerned that I would somehow injure her. Thankfully, both the suppository and fleet enema worked.

To keep things moving and grooving, here are some products that have helped mom and dad: Prune juice. Mom and Dad drink a half of a cup every morning and it makes a world of difference. I (at a doctor's suggestion) began administering Colace Stool Softener tablets when needed to mom. Fruits, especially kiwi, and vegetables, and a teaspoon of olive oil every few days. Another doctor suggested that mom and dad take a probiotic pill once or twice a week and water. My brother and sister-in-law sent both of our parents their own 64 ounce water bottles. And yes, I am the hydration police around the household. If they haven't had enough water, I absolutely notice and I absolutely get them on the "drinking water case." If mom seems extra tired on a given day, I look in the fridge and nine out of ten times, she hasn't had enough water. Water truly makes a world of difference re: the health and well-being of ourselves and our loved ones.

Now, because mom couldn't move her arm, she also couldn't scoot over. So, **getting her in and out of bed was a two-person job. Dad and I rigged a system where we put a towel underneath her. This way one of us would help mom get into bed and the other person (me)**

would pull the towel towards the center of the bed. We wanted to pull her a way from the edge of the mattress. We didn't want her falling out of bed in the middle of the night. Plus, the bed itself was a bit high. This had never been an issue, but when you're 5'4" with a broken arm, scooting is an issue. This towel method absolutely worked. If you use this method, my recommendation is that you pull from your core not just from your arms and shoulders. I say this because after about a month of doing this, I injured something in my shoulder. I actually felt it tear. And it continued to cause me shoulder problems for going on two years. So, pull from your core. I think the injury (my injury) also came because mom got up to go to the bathroom several times a night, which meant, dad and I had to wake up with her/help her. Sleep deprivation puts your body at risk. So, **sleep is also very important for the caregiver. We simply must make it a priority.** My shoulder was ultimately healed, by the way, through acupuncture.

About a week or two into the ordeal, I took mom back to TOA to see how the arm was looking. The doctor looked at and then rewrapped mom's wrist and arm. He suggested that she get a shot for pain relief. "And," he said, holding up a box that contained an arm sling. "Except when she's bathing or taking a shower, I want her to use an arm sling. The nurse will be in shortly to administer the pain meds and instruct you on how to use the arm sling." Now, the doctor had a nurse that just emanated anger. Dealing with her was tricky. But, as you might've noticed, I am not a passive caregiver. So, I was very aware of how each person was handling and talking to mom. The angry nurse stomped in, gave mom a quick jab of the pain medication and needless to say, her arm sling instruction was poor to nil. She just wasn't a kind or caring nurse, at least not in our experience of her. Happily, upon our return a few weeks later, I asked that we not have to deal with that particular nurse only to find out that the angry nurse no longer worked there. Hmmm, dare I say divine intervention?

Back to the journey, for the pain, they put mom on tramadol. The medication made her nauseous though. So, they switched her to OxyContin. Timing really is everything. For I had recently listened to a podcast about the opioid crisis. The podcast went into great detail re: how quickly a patient in pain can become a patient addicted to OxyContin. So, I was hyper-aware and watchful re: mom taking this particular drug. Here's what I found out through simple observation, mom's personality began to change. After about three weeks on oxy, she began to be, well, different than she'd ever been. She was aggressive in a way that just wasn't like our mom. At that point, I called one of the nurses at TOA and asked how to safely wean her off the OxyContin. The kind nurse gave me wise advice, and I immediately began tapering mom off the medication. Mom's arm was healing and steadily improving and, after the tapering, Tylenol seemed to do her just fine. OxyContin addiction averted.

One last piece of advice: **If an elderly loved one's arm has been broken, once the arm heals, moving forward,**

always put the recuperated arm into shirts and coats first. As a person struggles to get that second arm into a coat, it can put pressure on the arm as they reach back. **Takeaway: Why strain a previously injured arm? Put the once injured arm into the coat first and gently guide the other arm towards the arm hole of the coat. I have found this coat procedure quite helpful and I hope it helps you too.**

Schedule Your Own Self-Care

8

It's easy to lose yourself as you caretake others. The needs in front of you are immediate, necessary and never-ending. Still, I highly recommend scheduling time to do whatever makes you happy. Here's an example: I'm a writer. Writing is how I make sense out of life. So, a few months into the coronavirus journey, I applied to the UCLA Screenwriting Certificate Program. I figured if I was going to be stuck at home 24/7, I might as well spend my free time writing. UCLA offers a nine month intensive screenwriting certificate program in which the goal is to finish two feature length screenplays. What a wonderful program. Each week, there was a lecture, a question and answer class, and a screenwriting class. This meant that each week I had to generate script pages for class. The lectures, the classes, the writing, every second of this program was absolutely life-giving. And in the middle of all of the caregiving, it was just the thing to provide self-care for myself. The U.C.L.A. program gave me something of my own to focus on, which filled my cup as an artist, but also as a writing professor, I gained a deeper understanding of the craft, which in turn directly impacted the joy I feel as I teach my own writing classes. **What do you feel passionate about? Whatever it is, make time for it in your life.**

Now, UCLA was a bigger self-care project, but, on a smaller scale, after the UCLA certificate program ended, I made a pact with myself to take every Friday off from caregiving to write. That once a week break helped and helps me more than I can say. It also keeps me moving forward regarding my writing projects. For you, it might be going to an afternoon movie or taking a dance or pottery class. Whatever it is, do it. **Takeaway: Follow your passions while being a caregiver. This will keep your cup of fulfillment full.**

9

I think it's important to acknowledge that, if your family member is over seventy, people around them will begin to pass away. Mom's friend Ken from water aerobics took a tumble and the next thing we knew he was in hospice. We visited him regularly during his time at Alive Hospice. His wife Gerry, a precious, wonderful, water aerobic's friend of mom's was there and the three of us held conversations as a literal death rattle rattled every time Ken took a breath in the nearby bed. We attended his funeral and not long after, as these things sometimes go, we attended Gerry's funeral as well. In 2019, mom and I also regularly visited my godmother Belle at Alive Hospice. We went once, sometimes twice a week. Sang with her, prayed for her, just tried to be a loving presence and then, attended her funeral. It was a bit of a drive to Belle's funeral, but it was worth every mile to be there for Laura, my friend since fourth grade. **Showing up. Life is about showing up.**

In 2020, our family friend Mary died. Dean, Mary's husband, has been friends with dad since childhood. And Mom and dad had been friends with Dean and Mary throughout their entire marriage. I too loved Mary and was grateful for her gentle friendship to the Fischer family. It was an outside service and we all wondered how Dean would fare since he and Mary had the kind of connected marriage that other's hope for and aspire to. Thankfully, Dean is still thriving. I think the reason Dean is still thriving is because he makes it a practice to regularly serve others. From my experience keeping our eyes on others does tend to make life doubly meaningful.

Not long after Mary's death, dad's best friend Charlie was diagnosed with cancer and after doing all that could be done, he also passed away. That was such a terrible surprise. This country songwriting legend, over a decade younger than our dad, so full of life, wisdom and love, gone. The memorial was at our longtime friend Phil Vassar's house (also a country music legend) and being there was a gift. After going through the Covid lockdown, it was such a gift, getting to be around people, hugging people and connecting with people who loved Charlie as much as we did.

Mom's friend Bea, at one hundred years old, also died. Bea had been a constant in mom's life for years: playing cards and attending shows and events with a church group called "The Fun Bunch." And out of the blue, my prayer partner Ann experienced a brain bleed and not long after she too died. Ann was a fierce friend, and when she passed it was such a blow. She left an indelible mark in my life. Dad's incredible sisters Dolly and Pat passed during this time as well. And then, my cousin/mom and dad's niece, Kathy died. (More on these stories later.)

We were not strangers to loss as a family. Mom's father, Leo, her older brother Wayne, her closest brother Jack, her wonderful sister Mary, her dear sister Edna had been gone for quite sometime. Dad's dad died in a car wreck when dad was two. His mom died when he was newly married. Dad had (long before the Covid year) lost his older brother Dick, sister-in-law Mary, brother-in-law Duane, brother-in-law Jon and brother-in-law Don. So, death wasn't (sadly) a stranger. But still, each time an additional friend or family member passed, they left a hole in our hearts that only that family member or friend could fill. And midway through writing this book, dad's longtime buddy Austin Roberts, and his close friend Robert Lewis both passed away and mom's longtime friends Pauline and Dianne are both wading through dementia. All four of these friends, were and are near and dear to my parents. **Takeaway: Our society wants to hide this part of what happens. I say, dive in. Go and visit people, hug them, play music, sing together. And, if possible, go to your friend's and family member's funerals because their life, our lives, our shared history matters.**

10

Mom has always been particular about her hair. Throughout my life (and hers) she's gone to "beauty operators" on a regular basis. But once the pandemic struck, her hair was left to me. That said, I thought as a person who's never had one second of training, it might be useful to describe the method I came up with re: cutting and curling mom's hair. But before I go there, I want to first talk about something a lot of seniors deal with and that is an **itchy scalp. Whether it's caused by Psoriasis or dermatitis, or a fungus, I recommend Nizoral shampoo. The key is to leave the shampoo on for ten to twenty minutes. This is what mom's dermatologist recommended/what works for mom. I also (only when absolutely necessary) apply Fluocinonide Topical Solution USP 0.05% to mom's scalp. It's a strong corticosteroid medication. So, best not to use it for an extended period of time and best, as always, to consult a doctor before using it.** Also, if your family member can no longer get in and out of a tub or if using a shower has become dangerous for them, **I recommend that you ask your loved one's doctor if a bath bench might be**

helpful. A bath bench will allow your loved one to sit down and then scoot over and into the middle of the bench/tub. Getting in and out of a tub can be harrowing, especially when slippery from the water. The bath bench we bought has a back and the seat isn't slippery, which is great for safety reasons. Also, the bath bench does away with having to lower the person into the tub. You will also want to install a **handheld shower head** onto the bathtub faucet. I recommend that you buy water shoes, shorts or an outfit that you're okay getting wet in for yourself. If you have a helper even better. That person can stand outside the tub at the end of the bench while you stand behind the bench. Thus, keeping your loved one from falling backwards or sideways. The inside end of the bath bench has a handle that will help your loved one scoot themselves over on the bench while also keeping them from falling between the shower wall and the bench. I suggest that you put everything you'll need within reach: washcloths, face soap, body soap, lotion, shampoo, towels and a change of clothes. You don't want to leave your loved one unattended while you go in search of some product. Putting on good music is also a win.

As far as hairstyling for a female loved one goes, here's the method that works for me. Buy a pair of sharp scissors, small or medium curlers and a bonnet hair dryer. Once a month is hair cut day around our house. Here's how I do it. I take small amounts of hair and cut off about a half inch. Then, immediately put the trimmed hair into a curler. This is how I keep track re: what part has been cut and what part has not. I cut the same amount for each patch of hair. After putting the curlers in, I place the bonnet on mom's head, set the heat to medium or low depending on how it feels to her and let her sit under the dryer for a good 40-45 minutes. While she's under there, I usually bring her a snack as well. After her hair is dry, I take the curlers out starting at the bottom of her hair. This way, I can gently pull the curl out over the curl beneath it. No real brushing needed. Just a tiny bit of smoothing out a curl here or there, a bit of hair spray and her hair is looking good for days. If you're dealing with longer hair, then, I suggest using a medium to large round brush as you blow out your loved one's hair.

I also became dad's barber during Covid. For this, I bought a cordless hair trimmer/clipper. For the most part, I just follow the basic method shown on the manual. If you stick to the basics, you'll be fine. You can also look up men's hairstyles online. There are some terrific instructional hair styling videos on YouTube. **Takeaway: Nizoral shampoo for an itchy scalp (just be sure to leave the Nizoral on for at least 10 minutes before rinsing it off) and a bath bench, handheld shower head for bathing the elderly. For hairstyling: sharp scissors, curlers, a bonnet hair dryer and music, always music.**

11

I want to briefly address dud doctors. Both my parents had a doctor (who shall remain nameless) who was completely detached. She just didn't seem tuned in. They both liked her fine, but each time I attended a visit, my gut said that they weren't in good hands. Well, at one point, mom was having extreme pain whenever she sat down. I called the doctor wanting to get an x-ray, but the doctor was unavailable. Now, mom was in so much pain, I had no choice, but to become a squeaky wheel. "When would the doctor be available? Was there a way to get a message to her?" To say the least, the nurse was not happy with me. Finally, I said, "I think if this were your mother, you'd be doing exactly what I'm doing, asking questions and endeavoring to get results." After that, the nurse contacted the doctor and convinced her to call in an x-ray referral at TOA. The x-ray determined that mom had a **stress fracture on her tailbone.** When the results came back, even the nurse was in my corner. "You were right. Your mom did need an x-ray." She said.

Let me take a moment to say that our mom is one of the kindest people on the planet. She has been supportive towards me and my brother without pause. She is exactly who I aspire to be. And without hesitation, I will go to the ends of the earth to get this amazing woman the care that she needs.

For mom's tailbone stress fracture, I bought two things: a donut pillow and a raised toilet seat. The donut pillow provided relief while mom was seated and the raised toilet seat, provided extra height making it much easier for mom to get up and down from the toilet. It took a good 4-6 weeks for the injury to heal. Boy was I glad, I got mom scheduled for the x-ray, which put her on the path to recovery. It still nagged at me, however, that had I been complacent, mom would have had to wait through a long weekend before receiving the x-ray referral. This whole situation put a bug in my bonnet to find a new GP doctor for mom and dad. Finally, in 2021, I met, not only a doctor, but **a geriatric doctor**. As soon as I saw how very caring this doctor was, I was determined to sign my parents up with her. Her name is Dr. Monica Stout and she is a human being who makes the world a better place. When I first encountered Doctor Stout, she was full up with patients, but she had taken a liking to mom and as soon as she said yes to taking her on as a patient, I asked if dad could come along as well. She had met dad and been charmed by him and, hallelujah, she said yes to taking on both mom and dad as patients. The key factor is that she is a **geriatric doctor, which made all the difference**. She had insight into people going through the very things mom and dad would or might go through.

The dud doctor dilemma also arose re: mom's first neurologist (who shall also remain nameless.) Similarly, he just wasn't seeing our mom. He was seeing patient number 124. Over time, I got the impression that he didn't care about the elderly. This is a thing, a real thing. Doctors who are dismissive/ageist towards the elderly. He also didn't react well to my caretaker questions. After numerous disappointing encounters, I became vigilant and on the look out for a new neurologist. **Takeaway: If your loved one is elderly, consider switching them to a geriatric doctor.**

Gout, Foot Fungus and Ingrown Toenails

12

· ·

Overnight, one of dad's big toes became bright red, warm-to-the-touch, swollen and painful. We took him to the Vanderbilt walk-in clinic where the doctor told us it was gout. Gout is an inflammatory arthritis. Uric acid builds up and forms needle-like crystals in the joints. (Yikes!) The walk-in clinic doctor prescribed **Colchicine for dad's gout and it vastly improved his condition.** I suggest if your loved one's toe suddenly becomes bright red and tenderto-the touch, take them to a walk-in clinic. Not only is the condition extremely excruciating, if left untreated it can lead to other unwanted conditions like: lasting joint damage, bumps under the skin and kidney stones.

Another time, mom came down with a low grade fever. (99.9) I have no idea if the two were related, but she also had a very painful, infected ingrown toenail. The doctor clipped her toenail and put her on an antibiotic cream. Her low grade fever went away and her toe was on the mend in no time. This whole ordeal set me on a journey of regularly trimming mom's toenails, which was no easy task, but I didn't want her to find herself in pain with another ingrown toenail. So, I became her pedicurist. (Dad, at this point, seemed fine cutting his own toenails.) Each week, I would soak mom's feet in water and then trim her toenails. (More on toe care later.) **Takeaway: Take ingrown toenails seriously.**

13

Let's be honest, taking care of a loved one, especially a parent has its ups and downs. This is the person who has made you who you are or in my case these are the people who have made me who I am. They literally created the bulk of my emotional triggers and this can be, well, triggering at times. It can also be an opportunity to heal old, childhood wounds. But knowing that healing is on the horizon doesn't magically make all the moments easy. That's why, on the days when you find yourself clashing with your family member, rather than yelling at your loved one, I recommend going into an empty room and letting out a loud scream. Like taking the lid off a boiling pot of soup, it will take a bit of the pressure off the moment. This has helped me more times than I can count. For me, the goal is to become more patient over time, more accepting re: where they are physically, emotionally and psychologically. The caregiving road is full of love, connection and meaning, but it can also be a back alley that is full of frustrating, painful, upsetting potholes. Some of those potholes cause tears, some call for a massive need of patience, some cause huge amounts of sorrow. On the not-so-perfect days, rather than trying to control everything, go into a room and let off a little steam by yelling at the walls. **Remember your loved one was once in control of every detail of their life and now you're telling them what to do. That can't be easy for them.** You're asking them to walk with their walker or wait for you to help them get out to the car. It's for their safety, but no one likes to be told what to do. As they age, they might also forget precious memories, memories you need and want them to remember because those memories are your history/shared experiences. **Rather than trying to force someone to remember something that they no longer remember, just accept where they are and love them there.** You can also try showing them pictures to help jog their memory. Side note: My brother and sister-in-law just got mom and dad a **Nixplay frame. It's a preloaded digital frame and it's fabulous.** We keep it on all day and are regularly delighted to look up and see loved ones pop up in photos throughout the day. I highly recommend this as an option to keep loved ones that are faraway close, especially if memory issues are at play.

Whatever you do, remember you're on a journey and it is important for your own mental and emotional health to not fight what is. **It's important to accept where your loved one actually is on their journey and then, simply be with them there.** Here's an example: mom wrote a note on a card, but later, she didn't remember writing what she'd written. She didn't recognize her handwriting. So, she

51

wanted to write another note on the card. I could have tried to convince her that she'd already written on the card, but to what end? Why not just hand her a pen and let her write a second happy birthday on the card? I'm sure the person receiving the card would just think she had more to say and so wrote twice. No need to be right. No need to shame. No need to argue. **Takeaway: No matter what's going on, here's a guiding question and answer that I hope will prove helpful... What is the most loving response to the situation at hand? Whatever is most loving, do that.**

Games

14

· ·

Mom loves to play cards. Specifically, Rummy 500, but to play to five hundred takes a good bit of time. Instead, we play two hands of rummy a day (most days.) This entertains mom (and us) and also doesn't make every day only about cards. Whatever entertainment your loved one loves, I suggest touching base with it a few times a week. We also play Cat Bingo, which is bingo, just with cats on the bingo cards. Phase Ten and Farkle are also quite fun. Painting is a great way to spend an afternoon. In fact, I've painted numerous paint-by-numbers with mom. I highly recommend going online, getting a photo turned into a paint-by-numbers and then, painting that art project together. A few Christmases ago, mom, dad and I sat around the table making homemade ornaments. And for yet another Christmas, mom and I trekked to Brushfire Pottery Studio over the span of a few months and painted plates for six different family members, which was an absolutely wonderful experience. At other times, I break out a coloring book and we all tear out a page and color. Why? Well, first and foremost all of these activities are good for the brain and the spirit. So, why not give them a try? Do you own albums? If so, consider buying a portable record player and play music that your family member used to play/love. Or just type in music from the 50s, 60s, 70s, 80s, 90s etc. on Apple Music. My brother gave that tip and it's added so many joyful memories to our days. Music makes all the difference and singing is a fabulous activity. **Takeaway: Singing also uses the same muscles that we swallow with and, if like our mom, your loved one has trouble swallowing, this will strengthen the exact muscles that need to be strengthened.**

15

Once mom's arm healed, she got a referral for physical therapy. I was so happy that mom's arm would be stretched and strengthened. The physical therapist was a nice enough fellow. We went a few times and all was well. But on the last appointment (last because we stopped going) mom kept saying that the stretch he was doing on her arm hurt. He said, "That's normal." And maybe it was, but, when he stepped away, I asked mom, "Did the pain feel like workout pain or like bad pain?" She said, "It didn't feel like good pain." Once he returned to the table, I asked him to stop doing that particular stretch. He countered. I stood firm. He moved on to another stretch. It wasn't a terrible exchange. But, as we left, mom didn't want to schedule another appointment. This is a tricky one because **working out doesn't always feel good. But if the not feeling good feels more like harm than good, well, maybe stop doing that particular exercise or stretch or simply find another physical therapist.** I trusted mom's take on it all and, since she didn't want to return, we didn't return. **Takeaway: Listen to your loved one. If they**

communicate that something doesn't feel right, trust them.

Urinary Tract Infection Part One

16

Literally, out of the blue, Dad got sick with chills, nausea and a fever of 101.4. I kept track of it for a day, but, when he didn't seem to be getting better, I took him to the Vanderbilt walk-in clinic where Dad was diagnosed with a urinary tract infection. We got him on antibiotics and he was on the mend in no time. My wise sister-in-law Janet recommended cranberry juice, which absolutely helped him recover. UTI's are caused by a build up of bacteria. So, it's a good idea to monitor how often your loved one is bathing or showering. If left untreated, UTI's can lead to sepsis, which leads to death. Another sign of a UTI is confusion, btw. So, if someone suddenly has a fever or is acting confused, best to get them checked out A.S.A.P. **Takeaway: The thing about aging is, you can't mess around. Something small can become something large in no time. So, if the fever's not going away, go to the**

doctor. Also, I highly recommend, serving up a small glass of unsweetened cranberry juice on a regular basis. Cranberries, as it turns out, help to prevent bacteria from sticking to the bladder walls.

Gas

17

I'm a big believer in the product Gas-X. Why? Well, on numerous occasions mom and dad have had terrible stomach aches. Rather than panic, I hand them a Gas-X tablet, ask them to take it and tell me how they feel in thirty minutes. Nine out of ten times it works and thirty minutes later, they feel one hundred percent better. Gas-X contains simethicone, which helps to break up gas bubbles. Thus, enabling your body to get rid of trapped gas. **Takeaway: If your loved one is having gas related stomach pain, why not consult your doctor re: giving Gas-X a try?**

18

I had just gone for a walk. The weather was fabulous. So, I decided to water our peach tree. It was June 22, 2021 and I had no clue that everything was about to get totally turned upside down. Let me back up, I had been prompting, suggesting and outright begging mom to use her walker, but she just didn't want to use it. And I get it, a walker means you're old, a walker means you need help, a walker isn't a good look. But because of her Parkinson's, mom's gait was increasingly unsteady. And because she has osteoporosis, falls of any kind can lead to broken bones. Thus, my nagging her to use the walker.

I wasn't in the room when she fell. Evidently, she was standing up while trying to fold clothes, fell onto the side of the couch and cascaded down onto the floor. Dad called. (As I mentioned, I was in the front yard, hose in hand, about to water our peach tree.) As soon as I heard his voice, I knew something was terribly wrong. I bolted inside to find mom lying in a heap on the floor. "Can you get up?" "No." "Do you think something is broken?" "Yes." "911, we need an ambulance." We were still in Covid times. So, dad couldn't ride in the ambulance and both of us couldn't go into the ER, meaning only one of us could be with her at the hospital. The paramedics recommended that I stay behind and talk to the admitting manager on the phone while dad went to/waited at the hospital. I will never forget that phone call, getting asked questions that felt beyond my scope of understanding. Giving mom's insurance information and agreeing to things that I didn't totally understand. I did have the wherewithal to repeatedly get confirmation that mom's insurance would be covering the bulk of the bill and that I wasn't somehow putting my name down as a responsible party. This may sound paranoid, but some places sneak the term "joint several liability" and "responsible party" into contracts and then, try to force the caregiver or family member to pay for a loved one's medical bill. Strangely enough, I had just talked to a friend about that very topic. An assisted care facility had tried to force her to pay for overpriced expenses after her mother had gone into hospice and passed away. So, as I answered all of these questions, important questions re: our mom, I was filled with anxiety. Not to mention, the concern re: how mom was doing and what was happening at the hospital? After I got off the phone, dad called and filled me in. Mom's hip was broken and she was on the docket to have hip surgery. Dad stayed at the hospital while she was in the operating room. I stayed by the phone praying. Because of Covid, like I said, only one person could be with her at a time.

The next day, I relieved dad and then, spent the night with her in the hospital. She was, as you can imagine, pretty out of it. Thankfully, the surgery had gone well. Also, thankfully, a nurse asked me if I wanted mom to be on OxyContin or Tramadol? Knowing the dangers of Oxy, I responded "Tramadol" without hesitation. The next day, my wonderful brother Robbi and his great wife Janet and one of my fabulous nieces came into town and boy howdy, were we glad to see them. For the better part of a week, we all took turns visiting mom. It was such a relief to have family nearby, helping out. At one point, while they were all taking turns visiting with mom, I booked myself an appointment at a spa where I floated in a sensory deprivation tank, which was very relaxing. (I'd done it once before in Brooklyn so I knew what to expect.) Afterwards, I had dinner with a longtime friend. Does this sound like a luxurious day in the middle of total stress and mayhem? Yes, it does and yes, it was. It was also a wise choice. As I said, my brother and sister-in-law were in town to help. So, while they helped, I participated in some self-care. **No matter what's happening, remember to take care of yourself. Especially, if you're sleeping next to your loved one in the hospital.** Did I have to spend the rest of the nights, sleeping next to mom at the hospital after my brother, sister-in-law and niece left? No. But I know one thing for sure, the more present the family members are, the more likely nothing wonky will happen and the more excellent their care will be because they have an advocate right there in their room. Thankfully, the hospital provided a chair that reclined and I was actually able to sleep, even while hearing the constant beeps and buzzes and distant hallway voices in the hospital. On day seven, mom was ready to leave. The problem was where would she go? She still had to heal.

A word about the Ascension St. Thomas West staff. They were absolutely terrific. To expedite mom's discharge, I made it a point to make friends with the woman who was in charge of sending patients to aftercare facilities. Thankfully, the woman took a liking to me and once mom's main surgeon said she was ready to be released, the woman booked mom into the Woodcrest at Blakeford. Wasting no time, I dashed over to Woodcrest to set up mom's room at the rehab facility. I placed family photos in the room, dropped off some clothes and a few nightgowns for her to wear, and, of course, a deck of cards. And, after eight long days in the hospital, they released mom to move into the rehabilitation center.

The next five weeks, dad and I split our schedule. He would go to see her in the morning and I would visit in the afternoon. When mom was off doing physical therapy, I'd grade homework for my writing classes. When we were together, we'd watch TV or play cards. At night, dad, mom and I would watch *The Wheel of Fortune* together. (A show mom and dad have regularly enjoyed for years.) And each night when dad and I had to leave, it was excruciating.

Mom had never been apart from family. So, she had no desire to stay there without us. And yet, at 7:00 p.m., we had to go. There were a few Covid scares while she was there as well. Mom wasn't sick, but someone in the facility was. And so, during those times, dad and I would talk to mom through her window. To deal with this, I brought a folding chair and just left it outside her window so that, we could sit and talk with her through the window until the powers that be would let us resume our inside visits. All the while, mom wanted to come home. One night, she called me at one in the morning begging me to come and get her. Here's the thing that you don't find out (usually) until you're up against a situation like this. Your loved one can't come home until the rehab center says they're ready to be released. If your loved one leaves early, insurance might not pay for the time that was already spent in the rehab center. Also, you don't want your loved one home until they're ready anyway because you want them to be better, healed, able to resume life at home. In other words, the patient has to meet certain criteria to be able to leave. Benchmarks that when met, show that the patient will be able to operate in the outside world. (Believe you me, I was very inquisitive re: what those specific benchmarks were and I readily met with and informed the social worker, when mom had, at long last, met the requirements.) Still, to have my sweet mom calling, desperate to be out of there, was heart wrenching. She was also on pain meds and so not totally her regular self. I didn't argue with her. I didn't say no. I simply said, "Mom, I wish I could come get you, but they've locked the doors and I can't get in there right now, but dad will be there as soon as the doors open tomorrow morning."

By this point, I had graduated from the U.C.L.A. Certificate Program. But, by happenstance, I had signed up for a class through a wonderful screenwriting program called ProPath. I wanted to polish one of the scripts I had written while in the certification program. The timing was perfect and it kept me from being completely consumed by what was going on with mom. ProPath allowed me to focus on creativity during the week as well as my Lipscomb classes and being there for mom, which was a gift.

If the A story in this chapter is mom's broken hip, then, the B story is dad's injured toe. In the middle of all the rehab visits, dad had precariously balanced a large glass of apple juice in the freezer. The next time he opened the door the, now frozen, glass came tumbling down onto his big toe. It looked awful, red, swollen, painful. So, off to the walk-in clinic for x-rays we went. Thankfully, the x-ray showed no broken bones. But yowza, was he wobbling around for a while. The doctor prescribed rest and an antibiotic cream.

On the mom front, time steadily passed. Five weeks of time to be exact. And after five weeks (one week in the hospital and four weeks at the Blakeford) mom was headed back home. **To get ready for her, I purchased a new walker**. We also bought the **bath bench** that I mentioned in an earlier chapter. We installed **a hand held shower head**. Added a new **raised toilet seat** to her bathroom toilet and put **Medline Steel Folding Commodes** just off the porch as well as in mom and dad's bedroom, so that mom wouldn't have to hurry to the bathroom no matter where in the house she was. Didn't want any falls to occur during the day or night. We had **a hospital bed** delivered as well as **a new wheelchair**. As I mentioned previously, we already owned an old, hand-me-down wheelchair, but the new one gave mom a much smoother ride, which was important since even the slightest bump caused her physical distress. On a side note, we paid rental on the hospital bed and the wheelchair for a certain amount of time and after the prescribed time passed, we then, owned both the bed and the wheelchair. **Wanting to eliminate future fall risks, I removed all throw rugs. Poorly secured rugs, rugs that easily bunch or wrinkle are hazardous for the elderly.** Mom also had a new roster of **pills** to take post hip break. So, **I bought her a Walgreen's Seven Day Pill Organizer. This item was a Godsend as I endeavored to keep track of and administer all of mom's accumulating pills. Later, I bought two four pack 4PS Travel Pill Organizers. These pill organizers will change your life and I highly recommend them. They're easy to transport and can hold a whole day's worth of medications.**

One more part to the story, while in the hospital, they had diagnosed a blood clot in mom's heart, which led them to putting her on Eliquis, a medicine that reduces the risk of blood clots and strokes. (She was already on two blood pressure pills, Olmesartin and Diltiazem and Carbidopa

Levodopa for Parkinson's.) Lastly, **we had a ramp built** over the front porch by our handyman Port. This way mom could easily push her walker up to the front door. (Ramps can also be purchased on Amazon, if you don't have someone who can build one for you.) I then weatherized and painted the ramp with the hope that it would last for a long, long time. All of the above was quite a bit of work, but well-worth it for mom's care and safety. Once home, I immediately began weaning mom off the Tramadol. At this point, she'd been on pain meds for five weeks and her personality was becoming increasingly edgy. I'm happy to say that, after a few weeks of being off the pain medication, mom was more like her loving and lovely self. **Takeaway: Be sure to consult a medical professional before using any of the aforementioned products or when taking or tapering off any pain medications. If your loved one is unsteady on their feet, strongly encourage them to use their walker. And after a hip break, do everything you can to make the home safe for your loved one's return and, above all, don't precariously balance a glass of apple juice in the freezer.**

19

Within two days of her return, a Guardian home health nurse came by to evaluate and set up home nursing and physical therapy visits with mom, which was fabulous. How wonderful that she would be able to exercise and stretch her body after going through such an ordeal. Her physical therapist, Summer, was a gem and it was comforting, after being in the hospital and then rehab, to have a physical therapist to insure her continued strengthening progress as well as a home health nurse to check up on her health. We fell into a rhythm. Mom would have physical therapy once a week and a nursing visit once a week. After a while, the nursing part faded away and occupational therapy and speech therapy were added. The wise speech therapist recommended that mom sing.

Side note re: singing. Many Parkinson's patients develop swallowing problems. This problem causes the Parkinson patient to aspirate liquid and/or food particles into their lungs, which in turn can cause bacterial pneumonia. I know this because mom actually contracted bacterial pneumonia in August of 2021. The antibiotics

65

kicked it out of her system. But moving forward, I became very interested re: how to help mom's swallowing. And guess what? The speech therapist was right. **Singing strengthened mom's swallowing muscles.** Singing regularly works out well for us since (as I've mentioned) our dad is a songwriter and our mom knows all of his songs. I've often told dad how very lucky he is to have a wife who literally knows the lyrics to all of his songs. They are the perfect combo. He loves to write music and she loves to listen to and sing along to music. Mom was the kind of mother who often sang around the house and even to this day at age 89, she remembers lyrics like no one else, with the exception of my brother who remembers every song he's ever heard. Lol. All this said, dad, mom and I have continued, lo these many years, to sing four to five songs a day to keep mom's laryngeal muscles as strong as possible. Big thanks to the speech therapist for recommending that we regularly sing. Plus, music makes the house a more joyful place! **Straws can also be an immense help re: aspiration.** They change the way a person swallows, keeping them from aspirating. And one last trick: **If your loved one flies into a coughing fit when drinking a beverage, ask their doctor if having them dip their chin while swallowing might help. Dip the chin, water in, keep the chin dipped and swallow. Dip the chin, water in, swallow.**

Mom also developed a drooling issue around this time. This is because **Parkinson's patients swallow less, which**

causes a saliva build up and thus, a drooling problem. Two things that absolutely help with this: chewing gum and lozenges. Both remind the patient to swallow and drastically cut down on the drooling.

Back to mom's return from rehab… As I mentioned earlier, mom (and dad) now had a new fabulous geriatric physician named Dr. Monica Stout. So, we were able to check in with Dr. Stout soon after mom was released. Dr. Stout then scheduled my parents to see her every three months. What a caring doctor! On a father note, our dad (who was having **sinus issues**) was prescribed **Arm & Hammer Nasal Saline Spray, which dad found extremely helpful.** Doctor Stout also diagnosed mom with **lichen sclerosus**, a non-contagious skin condition, for which she was prescribed **Clobetasol. This product seemed to vastly help mom's skin condition. As you age, physical complications/reactions can compound and pile up. That said, Mom's immune system flared up, which caused an overall itchiness, also not contagious. For this, the doctor prescribed a medication for the treatment of neuropathic pain. Gabapentin changes the way nerves transmit messages to our brain. This "message lessening" reduces the itchy sensation. The medication also reduces anxiety.** Side note: Long-term use of the drug, however, is said, by Google, to cause cognitive impairment. It's one of those between a rock and a hard place scenarios. If your loved one is feeling an itchy sensation all over their body the medication absolutely helps with that. On the other hand, over time, memory loss is a potential risk factor. As I've mentioned throughout this book, I'm not an expert or a physician, I just know that various products that doctors have suggested or prescribed have helped my parents at various points along their aging journey. Please consult your doctor before using Gabapentin or any other drug mentioned in this book.

Big thanks to Dr. Stout who gave so much good advice, compassion and help along the way. She was an absolute gift in our lives. (I say "was" because, sadly, in 2023, Dr. Stout moved out of state. She did recommend/set us up with another lovely geriatric doctor before leaving though.)

Back to the story: Post rehab, mom also met with her hip surgeon on numerous occasions. And on one of those visits, he told us that mom's hip no longer showed a fracture. What wonderful news to hear that mom's hip had healed. On the downside, she was still feeling a good amount of pain. To remedy the pain, we were sent to another doctor who scheduled mom for a steroid shot. It was a simple, but stressful procedure for mom. Yes, it was just a shot, but the location of the shot was a bit tricky. When they wheeled her away from me, I felt a jolt of panic. What could I do though, but sit in the waiting room and pray for good results? Once the procedure was over and we were on our way home, we both sighed a deep sigh of relief. And on a good news note, the steroid shot worked and mom's hip felt immeasurably better within days. Can I get a hallelujah?! **Takeaway: Quick bit of advice about physical therapy. When you take your loved one for a checkup, see if they're eligible insurance-wise for physical Therapy. And sing, even if you're not a singer, sing loud and sing often.**

Communion & More Hospice

20

During the rehab stint, mom's Catholic Church sent Denise, a kind communion volunteer to pray with and administer communion once a week to mom. Talk about full circle. Back in the day, mom had done this very thing, bringing church to parishioner's apartments, hospital rooms and homes. Denise was so kind and her friendship with and prayers and care for mom was palpable. And the good news is, Denise has continued visiting mom even to this day. I highly recommend looking into church programs that have an outreach arm for/towards the elderly. Denise's visits have brightened mom's days and been such an ongoing spiritual encouragement in mom's life.

On a sad note, not long after mom returned from rehab, two of dad's three sisters went into hospice. (I also mention this in an earlier chapter.) Dolly and Pat were such loving forces in the life of our family. And knowing they were entering their last days was a blow. It was especially hard because there was no way we could go to visit them at this particular time. Thankfully, FaceTime had increased in popularity. So, we were able to see and speak to dad's sister Dolly on FT. And his big sister Pat had a **Grandpad Senior Tablet with phone capabilities**, which enabled dad to talk to and see his sister Pat regularly as well. As they advertise on their website, Grandpads offer an "easy approach to sophisticated tech." My Aunt Pat had an essential tremor , which caused her hands to shake at times, but even so, she was able to use her Grandpad to call family/see family on the screen. Especially for our dad, these conversations with both sisters were a lifeline.
Takeaway: Life is so precarious and precious. This is why we must, in my opinion, keep the channels between us open and connect.

21

In early 2022, I noticed that mom was regularly getting **out of breath**. We booked an appointment with mom's heart doctor, Dr. Rankin, and he put mom on **Spironolactone** 25 mg. Spironolactone is a diuretic that is used to treat fluid buildup. In other words, it helps the kidneys remove fluid and salt from the system. The medication absolutely worked and mom's breathing issue went away. A few years later, however, mom was dealing with a general loss of energy/fatigue, which is, on the downside, a side effect of the drug. So, for the next year and a half, mom got off Spironolactone and her energy level increased. Sadly though, mid-way through 2024, mom experienced on-going fluid retention/edema around her ankles and so her heart doctor put her back on Spironolactone. She no longer has fluid retention, but, once again, deals with fatigue. So, be sure to consult a medical professional about the use of the aforementioned drug. Another thing that **helps with edema are pressure socks. Pressure socks apply gentle pressure to the legs and feet, which increases blood flow. Takeaway: If your**

loved one's ankles are swollen, put on some pressure socks, and the swelling will substantially lessen.

Bone Density

22

. . . .

As I mentioned before, our mom has osteoporosis. So, in 2020, to strengthen her bones, she was prescribed a bone density increasing drug called Evenity. The regimen required that she get an injection once a month. So, once a month, we would trudge over to see mom's excellent and kind rheumatologist, Dr. Christian Rhea. And at the end of the year, mom's bone density had increased by 17%. Not only that, her bone density had returned to what it was in 2008. After the Evenity year was up, the rheumatologist prescribed Prolia, another bone density increasing drug. The regimen for Prolia requires that mom get an injection every six months. This drug has also worked and has, thus far, increased mom's bone density by 10.7% with (to our knowledge) no side effects. I bring these medications up in case someone you love is speaking with their doctor re:

bone density building options. **Takeaway: Evenity and Prolia increased mom's bone density.**

23

All during 2020-2021, I continued to write as much as possible. One of my creative outlets was with the Theatre East Writer's Group. As I previously mentioned, I had performed with them and they had produced my full-length play *Petie* as well as my two ten-minute plays:, *Jumping Up & Down Happy Town* and *Audition Class with Director Dash*. Being a part of their writer's group was a life saver during the pandemic. We met over zoom and all of the playwrights brought in pages of whatever project/play they were working on. The feedback from that particular group of writers was stellar and listening to their work was equally inspiring. It also filled a spot in my creative life that had previously been occupied by the Pipeline-Collective Salon and the Tennessee Playwrights Studio, two in-person writing groups that I had attended pre-pandemic. The great thing about writing groups whether they are live or over zoom is they get you out of your head and onto the page because you have committed to bring in pages. For example, while I was a member of TPS, I wrote the first draft of my play *Sunshine Madness*. And while I was a Dramatists Guild Fellow, I wrote the first draft of my (and Don Chaffer's) musical *The Sparkley Clean Funeral Singers*. These aforementioned groups were monumental in my creative life because I either finished drafts or improved drafts while being a part of them. If you're a writer, I hope you'll do everything you can to get the first draft of your play, screenplay or novel written. It doesn't have to be perfect. So, don't get hung up on perfection. Just make a commitment to yourself to get that first flush of the story out. If this seems impossible on your own, apply to, join or start a writers group. If you're not a writer, what is your equivalent passion? What project calls out to you?

Takeaway: Find ways to feed your soul while you feed, bathe, entertain and nurture others.

24

In October of '21, mom was fitted for hearing aids. They were very expensive and, quite frankly, worth every penny because they made a world of difference in mom's daily life. **Hearing, being able to hear, creates more brain activity, which in turn is good for the brain.** Also, **hearing loss and dementia are connected.** This doesn't mean a person will definitely get dementia if they have hearing loss, but it does mean that there is a connection and that that connection should be taken seriously.

While we're on the topic of hearing aids, I want to mention the words **proactive persistence**. After three years of use, mom's hearing aids were in need of some repair. So, in 2024, we took them to mom's Hearing Specialist. The specialist checked the hearing aids out and said she'd send them off to get fixed and that it would take seven to ten days. Two weeks passed, then, another two. So, I called and found out that mom's hearing aids were "missing." Evidently, that particular Hearing Specialist (who shall remain nameless) had abruptly quit, leaving no trace of mom's hearing aids. They referred me to another office. Nothing happened. I called back and in a calm, but firm voice I said to the receptionist, "My mom has now been without her hearing aids for well over a month. I want to know where her hearing aids are, what's going on and when we can speak to someone?" Time passed. I called again and said to the same rather pleasant receptionist, "I think you're lovely, but I want to be clear, I will call the office every day, if necessary. I will call and keep calling until mom's hearing aids are found, fixed and returned." The next day, a lovely new Hearing Specialist rang me up. She'd found mom's hearing aids, but they were yet to be fixed. Even so, she set up an appointment during which she gave mom some interim hearing aids to wear while we waited. Another month passed, but at least, mom could wear the interim hearing aids while waiting. Eventually, mom's hearing aids were fixed. I bring this story up because, **as a caregiver, you're gonna need to cultivate a proactive persistence on behalf of your loved one/s.** In the above story, I never raised my voice, no angry words were spoken, but I also wasn't sitting back waiting for the phone to ring. I'm convinced that, had I not called, mom's hearing aids would still be sitting in some unmarked box on some forgotten shelf waiting to be fixed. **Takeaway: Hearing aids are worth the cost/money. They increase brain activity as well as providing better hearing.**

25

October 2021 was difficult. Mom was feeling generalized anxiety. (She was ultimately prescribed a low dose anxiolytic medication for this, which helped.) But she was also a bit blue and argumentative. There was a role reversal at play. I was having to parent and we both were uncomfortable with our roles being reversed. My lifelong triggers were getting triggered and I didn't know what to do. Then, my longtime friend Suzanne gave me some expert advice. **"Just say yes." In other words, instead of trying to explain why something doesn't make sense or can't be done, just affirm your loved one. It doesn't mean lie. It just means don't try to correct or fix every discrepancy. They are your mother or father and they used to tell you everything. You used to follow their instructions and it can't be easy being on the receiving end of being taken care of rather than caretaking.** Big thanks to Suzanne who made my life so much easier by giving that one bit of great advice. **"Just say yes."** Suzanne knew this sage advice because her dad, who has since passed, had been diagnosed with Parkinson's at a way too early age. So, she had experienced some of the things I was experiencing and she knew things that I needed to know. One other gift she gave me was to prepare me for times when my mom might not be present enough to mother me. Thankfully, our mom, even to this day, is the first person to stretch out her arms and give out hugs, but there have been moments when she's been deep in her Parkinson's or hung up by anxiety or just, for whatever reason, unable to see past what her life has become. During these times, it's painful and difficult that this lifelong great caregiver, my original caretaker isn't available to simply care for/mother me. On those days, oh, how I miss the mom that I knew and know. My brother would agree we hit the jackpot by having our mom as our mom. She has been a lifelong giver. So, on the days, she's darted down a rabbit hole, so to speak, I take time to remember the past and the many times she listened to, comforted, uplifted and encouraged me. This helps me keep the whole picture in perspective. **Takeaway: Just say yes.**

26

On October 26, 2021, dad, who has always been an expert driver, was turning his car around and ended up with one wheel off the driveway. This made the bottom of the car flush with the concrete. (Yikes!) Thankfully, I had recently met and hired, Port Moore, a fix it guy. Port had rebuilt not one, not two, but three of our floors after we discovered termite damage. He had also fixed doors, windows, you name it. So, not knowing what to do, I called Port. And let me just say, that man rigged a ramp under the suspended back tire and got dad's car back on the driveway where it belonged. Talk about relief. This was also a turning point for dad re: parking under the carport. It's a tight space and you have to turn the car around and, as I mentioned in an earlier chapter, there's a considerable drop off on one side. The good news is, we have a circular driveway in front of the house as well. So, dad opted to keep his car there after the "one wheel off the driveway" episode. Dad also stopped, for the most part, driving at night around this time. No one harangued him. It was a conclusion he came to on his own. **Takeaway: Find a handyman or woman and keep them on speed dial.**

27

One thing that was a great comfort to me as I went through all of the experiences I've so far described was a friend of mine (who shall remain nameless.) On Saturday mornings, we would go for a walk and unpack what had happened over the previous week. Words can't capture how much I love this friend and how helpful those walks were. Our parents are humans with their own sets of strengths and flaws. And those strengths and flaws form us into our particular version of strengths and flaws. So, **it's only natural that returning home to help family would pose the question, "Will I succumb to past wounds or finally, at long last, heal them?" If you opt for healing, it's not a straight to the finish line trek. It's difficult work with wild curves. It involves forgiveness (of yourself and others) and it takes time.** Not every moment over the last five years has been handled with grace. And many times, I have felt frustrated by my many failures. But I would go on walks with this particular friend, and just having someone to describe what I was going through, helped me immeasurably. As I've mentioned, my goal is to become the best artist that I personally can be and, as a human steadily become the best and wisest version of myself as well. Part of becoming the best version of oneself is admitting when we're completely off the mark. Assessing our weaknesses rather than hiding them. And this friend was someone I felt safe with, safe to admit my less than perfect attempts. Throughout our relationship history, two things marked our friendship: First, we had soul chemistry, meaning we could talk and laugh for hours. Secondly, he often canceled our plans last minute. However, for many years, the soul chemistry and laughter outweighed the last minute cancellations. And once I discovered my love for acting, I moved to New York City, which meant we didn't talk to or see each other as much. But we did, even with all those miles between us, continue to support each other via the telephone. And when I'd come to town, we'd find time to grab a meal and catch up. He was my sounding board. I told him everything. His wisdom, his unique perspectives were invaluable. He helped me through my artistic and personal lows and celebrated the personal and artistic highs. When my musical *Barbara's Blue Kitchen* got produced Off-Broadway, he flew to NYC to see it. When his mom died, I hopped on a bus so that I could be there to support him. We had what I would call a thriving friendship. I loved him with an open heart and often prayed for his happiness and was thrilled for him when he met and married his life partner. I recount all of this and even as I recount it, it doesn't capture how very connected I felt to this friend and how seemingly connected he felt to me. I will always be grateful for all of the years I called him friend.

The second element though, the last minute cancellations became more prevalent once I moved back to Nashville. He would repeatedly and regularly cancel our walks last minute. It felt crappy on the receiving end and it was also a bummer because I couldn't then make other plans because it had been a last minute cancellation. People cancel, I get that. Things come up. I'm fine with that, but repeatedly canceling last minute shows a lack of respect for the other person's time. So, I took a risk one Saturday by asking that he no longer cancel last minute. Who knows why asking this ended the friendship, but it did. He accused me of being controlling, which was ironic because he was the one who said if we'd walk, when we'd walk, how long we would walk and then reserve the right to cancel our scheduled walks last minute. He didn't verbally say the friendship was over, he just ghosted me.

I had never imagined my life without that particular friend and it was, hands down, the biggest heartbreak of my life. And believe me, I've had a considerable amount of heartbreak. But to live my life without this friend, I just never saw that coming. It was confusing. It was jarring. It was especially difficult because as a caregiver, I no longer had his love and support as I tried to hold it all together for my parents. Simultaneously, I believe, it was also necessary that I would, for my own personal growth, stand up for myself and ask that my time be valued. It took me the better part of a year to grieve that friend's loss, but I also had to face the fact that he was okay without me and I needed to accept that and find ways to find joy regardless. I'm not perfect. There were most definitely other unseen factors at work, but he never expressed those unseen factors to me. So, I wasn't given the chance to be a better friend, talk things out and if need be, ask forgiveness. If the friendship had to end, I deserved a better ending. (And if someone has ghosted you, you didn't deserve it and you deserved a better ending too.) Still, I wish him well. He was there for me as best he could be for many a year and I wish him well. And even now, if he wanted to find a way to rebuild the friendship, without last minute cancellations, I would be open to giving a renewal of the friendship a try.

The above story compels me to bring up a tangential topic. **Some people do not like to talk about or be around sick, ailing or elderly people.** I doubt that this is why the aforementioned friendship went off the rails. But I do know, as a caregiver, you're bound to shed a few friends here and there because our society has a difficult time with sickness, frailty, aging and death.

Takeaway: Sometimes people leave you when you need them most. When or if this happens, I encourage you to move towards acceptance of the situation as quickly as possible. Staying in a dysfunctional idea, holding onto what was, will only cause more pain. I believe that holding onto an idea of who they are or were will only keep you stuck in the drama and pain.

28

On November 24, 2021, mom met with a cataract surgeon to discuss cataract surgery. Her eyesight had steadily gotten worse and so here we were getting instructions re: how to prepare for surgery and what to do post surgery. We left with prescriptions and instructions that I begin administering eye drops to mom pre-surgery. It was nerve wracking. Understandably, she kept blinking every time I tried to give her the eye drops. So, I had to find a way to gently hold her eye open. I stayed vigilant and somehow, someway, we got those drops in. Upon our arrival on the day of the surgery, they wheeled mom in to get her right eye done. She was pretty calm, but I was in a constant state of prayer as I sat in the waiting room as I'm sure dad was as well. I'd brought a book to read. Read the same sentences over and over with nothing sinking in. Then, went back to prayer and, thankfully, in less than an hour, my phone buzzed with a text saying, mom was ready to be picked up. Dad got the car, we loaded mom into her seat and headed home. The day after the operation, mom was scheduled for an appointment with her regular eye doctor. The news was absolutely encouraging. Mom's eye, just one day later, already had better vision. I don't know how people that live alone get through something like this because the eye drop regimen post-op is quite intense. There are numerous kinds of eye drops and the drops have to be put in at certain times, numerous times a day. Plus, it goes on for a full month, tapering off as you near the end. Two weeks later we were back at the Eye Center to get mom's left eye done. My brother and sister-in-law were in town this go-round, which was wonderful. And like the time before, mom's surgery went textbook smooth. I continued to put drops into the right eye and added on another month of me administering eye drops to mom's left eye and by the end of it all, I had become quite adept at eye drop application. Needless to say, it was all worth it because as time passed mom's vision got even better. She still uses glasses to read, but mom now has 20/20 vision. As I've previously said, modern medicine is amazing.

About a year after mom's cataract surgeries, mom developed a bit of scar tissue on one eye and had to go back to the cataract surgeon. Thankfully, he was able to remove the scar tissue without a problem. I include this bit of information to let you know that this can occur post surgery. **Takeaway: If your loved one goes in for cataract surgery, take all of the eye drop applications seriously and administer them on time.**

29

....

I started 2022 by co-writing a song titled *Shoveling Smoke* with dad and Craig, a fellow songwriter. We were all three quite happy with what we'd created and Craig promised to record a demo and then, send it along in a month or so. That same week, it snowed, which caused my gazebo to cave in. The day of the gazebo cave-in, I'd gone out into the gazebo to read for a while, but because it was quite cold out, I'd decided to go back inside the house. Had I stayed, I might very well be dead because the very place where I had sat just hours before was now crushed under the weight of the ice that had accumulated on top of the gazebo. To celebrate surviving, I caught up with my prayer partner Christina. What an amazing force of nature this prayer warrior is. How fortunate I am to call her friend. **Praying with prayer partners and sharing our life stories is a great support and help.**

As the freezing month of January 2022 dragged on, the snow outside our door piled up. When it snows in Nashville, the roads stay icy and driving can be hazardous. So, we were stuck at home. Rather than go stir-crazy, I decided to stir up an art project by hosting a play reading of my comedy *Greener Pastures* over zoom. I thought, "I might be snowbound, but that doesn't mean I can't bond with fellow artists." The actors were terrific. And afterwards, I promptly plunged into a script tweak. As I've mentioned, writing is at all times a salve to my soul. So, sitting in a comfy chair working on my comedy *Greener Pastures* was a perfect way to spend my time. And as the year crept into February, I found myself in a loop: caretake, write, grade homework, repeat, caretake, write, grade homework, repeat. One good thing, one fun thing, one satisfying thing, one hard thing, one soul replenishing thing, one good thing.

Also during this time, I created a website for our dad. www.bobbyfischersongwriter.com He loved it. My kind, caring, talented, hilarious dad is truly my favorite songwriter. So, creating a website for him was the perfect gift. **Is there something that your loved one does that might require a website? If yes, I suggest that you set one up. They can put their poems or stories or songs etc. on their site and hand out cards to the various people that they meet.** It will add a new dimension to their life. (Yes, I had business cards made for dad as well, and yes, he gives them out to every person he encounters. What can I say? He's a songwriter who wants people to hear his songs.)

In March, my parent's dear friend Dianne popped into town with her daughter Libbie and Libbie's husband. Oh, how quickly things can change. When we saw Dianne in 2019, she was sharp as a tack. And now, a mere three years later, this singer, this loving, smart artist and caring, wise family friend had full on dementia. Life sure does throw a lot of curve balls. This brings me back to our song *Shoveling Smoke* and the demo that Craig was going to make. After a long stretch of not hearing from this brilliant songwriter, I learned that he had quite suddenly passed away. Here was this guy, forty maybe? A full of life, extremely talented musician who was now gone. None of us know how long we have, or how many disasters have been averted (ie the gazebo collapse.) **Takeaway: Best to make the most of every day and love the people in front of us rather than nitpick them or miss the moments by longing for the past or only focusing on the future. "Be here now" is a wise saying for a reason. Oh, and don't sit under any ice covered gazebos.**

30

If your loved one sleeps in a hospital bed at home or on an angled bed, in preparation for any family trips, send a wedge pillow to the location where you will be staying. And if they have balance issues, buy and send a bedside commode ahead as well. This way, your loved one can sleep on an angle and not have to walk far for bathroom needs in the middle of the night. I also recommend a deck of cards. If your flight is delayed, this will help pass the time. And finally, when flying, don't check your loved one's walker. Bring it to the gate and check it as you board the plane. This way, this much needed cargo, won't get lost or left behind. Oh, and carry all medication onto the plane. **Takeaway: Send necessary items ahead when traveling and, when flying, take your loved one's walker to the gate and check it as you board the plane.**

31

....

I had repeatedly heard from medical professionals that I should get mom and dad's advanced directives filled out. So, all three of us booked an appointment with a law firm where we got our wills drawn up and our advanced directives filled out, something I highly recommend that you do as well. It's also a good idea to laminate those advanced directives and carry them in your car. That way, you can present doctors, or emergency room workers with your loved one's wishes in times of crisis. Doctors are trained to do whatever it takes to keep people alive, but in worst case scenarios, you want what your loved one wants. So, don't leave things to chance. Be prepared because when dire moments occur, they almost always occur when you least expect them. I also recommend the book *The Art of Dying Well* by Katy Butler. This book is chock-full of insights/advice re: aging and preparing for death. Dire title I know, but better to be prepared rather than unprepared.

Speaking of all things dire… I want to talk for a moment about crooks who prey on the elderly. As a caregiver, be on the lookout for scammers, liars and frauds who want to dupe older citizens. Some people have no problem stealing or scamming seniors. **Takeaway: Be vigilant and watch out for people who prey on the elderly. And no matter what age you are, getting a will drawn up is a good idea.**

Two Broken Ribs & Two Compression Fractures

32

My sweet mom likes to be in the middle of things. I love this about her. So, it was no surprise when I was about to mow the lawn and mom wanted to watch. So, dad brought her out, locked the brakes and situated mom on her seated walker. Here's the thing that a lot of people don't know, the thing we didn't know, **walkers can tip over. So, don't have your loved one sit on their walker.** I had hurried to the side of the house to get the lawnmower, which took less than twenty seconds and, as I rounded the corner, to my horror, mom was splayed out backwards on the grass. It was the worst. She had fallen backwards onto the lawn. I mention the lawn because it would have been catastrophic had she fallen backwards onto our concrete driveway. I asked her questions as I tried to suss out the damage. Then, came to the conclusion that she should stay put. I called an ambulance and they whisked her off to the hospital with me following along in the car. Dad stayed home since I knew it would be a long night. In retrospect, I wish he'd come along for moral support. But since he's also elderly, I was watching out for him by having him stay. Once in an emergency room, they put a cervical collar on mom's neck and started an IV line. They were not giving her fluids or meds at this time, but they had an IV line put in "just in case." The ER doctor, came in examined her and talked to us a bit. He then ordered some tests. Now, mom had fallen onto her back and it was her back that was hurting. She had not injured her head. I mention this because after a while, a radiographer came in and said, she was going to take mom to get a CT scan on her head. I said, "It's her back that's been injured." The radiographer, was immediately angry that I had questioned her, snapped, "It's for her head." I stood my ground. "It's her back that is hurting. That's what we discussed with the doctor." "The CT scan is for her head." She escalated. "Would you please double check with the doctor because it's her back that is in pain." I firmly replied. Now, let me be clear, if the doctor wanted a CT scan on both her head and back, I wouldn't have spoken up, but I knew darn well that we needed to know what was going on with her spine and, according to mom, her head wasn't hurting at all. The radiographer returned. No apology just, "Mrs. Fischer, I'm here to take you for a CT scan on your back." Again, if they wanted to do both so be it, but I spoke up because I didn't want to leave the hospital not knowing what had happened to mom's spine. **Here's the tough truth about being someone's advocate: you're not going to win any popularity contests doing it. People don't like to be questioned, even if your questions are on behalf of someone else, but ask questions anyway. Studies say that people who have advocates with them at the doctor's office or in the hospital get better care.**

After a short time, the surly woman brought mom back and then, mom and I waited for a VERY LONG TIME. The time factor comes into play because both the neck collar and IV line were causing mom a great deal of discomfort. She kept wanting to take them off/out, but the nursing staff was adamant that they were to stay on/in. Finally, at three in the morning, the ER doctor returned with the news that mom had incurred two broken ribs and two compression fractures in her spine. "You can go home or stay here. Do you want to be admitted for the night?" The doctor asked. "NO." Mom quickly replied. They removed the cervical collar and the IV line, released her and off we went, towards home and towards healing.

I want to take a moment to acknowledge that seeing your mother injured on the ground is traumatizing. Watching your father have a heart attack is traumatizing. So, you might want to **regularly incorporate coping strategies**. Definitely find time to exercise. Eat healthy food. Talk to trusted friends or a therapist and practice relaxation. The roller coaster that is caregiving is the main reason I schedule my writing time every week. And it's the main reason I want to encourage you to **take time out to do whatever soothes your soul**. Your loved one needs to heal, but you might need to do some healing as well. Living with the knowledge that something bad could and might happen at any moment is stressful. One thing I find helpful is talking to other caregivers. So, every once in a while, I touch base with my longtime friend Robin. Robin and I went to grad school together. She is a fabulous person/ screenwriter. And as it turns out, Robin is currently caring for her parents as well, which is why we always have a lot to discuss. I also often call my cousin Candace. She is always ready with an empathetic ear and sage advice. **Takeaway: What eases your mind? What helps you reset? What brings you joy? Whatever it is, schedule regular time for that activity. Also, don't try to soldier on alone. Reach out to loved ones who are wise counselors/ supportive friends.**

33

Ironically, on the day mom fell backwards, she had had physical therapy. (She had gotten another round of physical and speech therapy because her neurologist had tweaked her medications, which can sometimes allow for more in-home help.) **When it comes to broken ribs and compression fractures though, you mainly just have to rest/let them heal**. So, sadly, mom's PT had to fall by the wayside, while her bones repaired. The prescribed speech therapy, however, continued. I was especially grateful to mom's speech therapist this go-round because mom was, once again, having increased difficulty when swallowing and the new vocal exercises (along with our daily singing) absolutely helped mom out. We (mom, dad and I) also started doing **eye exercises, face exercises and tongue stretches. Parkinson patients can sometimes develop a non-expressive face. Face exercises strengthen the facial muscles and tongue exercises are helpful re: speech.** As we did all of this, time ticked along and little by little, mom made her way through the healing of the compression and rib fractures and her swallowing muscles became stronger, which brought her to a better place. She still has to be careful when she swallows, (fluid in, dip the chin, swallow) but she's not going into coughing fits/ aspirating as much. **Takeaway: Consider incorporating eye, face and tongue exercises.**

Eat Healthy, Go to the Gym & Hydrate

34

· ·

Update re: dad's heart: Miraculously, ever since his heart attack/getting two stents put in, dad has been energetic and strong. I wonder if part of his energy source is his upbeat attitude? He's just an all-round positive guy. **Here are some things that both my parents began doing in 2022 that I think contributes to their energy and longevity. They go to the gym six to seven times a week.** At the gym, they do a twenty minute workout. (Walking to and from the car, ten minutes on the recliner bike, a lap around the track, 5 minutes on the upper body ergometer/hand cycle, and then, a walk back to the car.) I believe that going to the gym as well as having a place to go is good for their physical, emotional and mental health. As a person ages, work ends and appointments (other than doctor visits) fall away. This creates a hole in the schedule. So, my parents have created a daily appointment that gets them out of the house and to the gym, which we all know is good for the body. **They also, as I've mentioned, hydrate, hydrate, hydrate**. I make them meals that are chockfull of **fruits and vegetables** and I regularly incorporate **beans and lentils**. We eat red meat, but, ever since dad's heart attack, only a few times a month. So, the **main protein** source would be **turkey, chicken and occasionally fish**. (Dad's not big on fish.) They also give best efforts **to not snack after 7:00 pm**. This gives their bodies a good ten to eleven hours to focus on something other than digestion. **Takeaway: Be like my parents and go to the gym.**

Urinary Tract Infection Part Two

35

· ·

Mom didn't feel well, had a slight temperature and her back hurt. I took her to a walk-in clinic where they obtained a urine sample and x-rayed her back. I was never quite clear why, but the physician recommended that we go to the ER. Here's the thing that's hard to know when you're dealing with the elderly, how bad or good are they actually doing? What I mean is, mom didn't feel great, but she didn't feel like she was at death's door either. But the physician, was pressuring me to whisk her off to the hospital. I didn't want to make the wrong call, so, even though mom was ambivalent about going, I checked her into the ER. In retrospect, we did not need to go to the ER this go-round. The ER did the exact same tests that the walk-in clinic had done and both places gave the exact same diagnosis: mom had a UTI and a new compression fracture. The previous compression fractures had put pressure on her back and most likely caused a new compression fracture to occur. Sadly, the location of this new compression fracture has made it difficult for her to stand up straight. Re: the UTI, mom was prescribed Nitrofurantoin, which worked.

Also around this time, Dad took a tumble. (These two senior citizens sure do keep me hopping!) He was taking the trash out and boom, he fell down onto the road. Thankfully, there was no on-coming traffic at that time! Doctor Stout scheduled dad for x-rays after which we found out that nothing was broken. (Yay!) On the downside, he was diagnosed with increased arthritis in his back. **Takeaway: Here are some products we've used to soothe dad's back pain over the years: Salonpas, Voltaren Arthritis Pain Gel, Bio-freeze pain relief roll-on Menthol, Lidocaine Pain Relief Patches. If your loved** one is experiencing chronic back pain, you might want to check in with their doctor to see if any of the aforementioned products might be of help.

Acupuncture, Massages, Fasting & Prayer

36

. . . .

A short word about acupuncture. In my experience, it works. I don't go regularly, but when my back gets mega tight or if something continues to bother me, I book an appointment with an acupuncturist and I always leave feeling better. I feel the same way about massages. They work for me. So, whenever possible, I get one.

As a caregiver, I'm hyper aware when I feel even the slightest sniffle since I don't want to pass along any viruses to my precious parents. But when I do feel under the weather, I drink tons of water, I take zinc and I fast for twenty-four hours. Digestion takes a lot of energy. So, I give my body a chance to simply heal. I also sleep as much as possible and add a bit of apple cider vinegar to my water a few times a day. I have thwarted a cold more times than I can count by doing these aforementioned things. Again, I'm not a doctor, but, for me, these things work.

On another note, I've mentioned prayer and prayer partners a good amount in this book. Here's a sample of something I might pray. "Lord, maker of the zebra, butterflies and everything green, be a cover of comfort over my friend who is grieving." Or, "Father, please give the surgeon a great night's sleep before my friend's surgery tomorrow." I might also just pray, "Help." I believe in a God who listens. I believe in a God who cares and so I find myself verbally reaching out to the One who thought up "mountains" on a regular basis. My favorite prayers are mom and dad's. Why? They don't get all fancy. They just mention basic needs. Mom often prays for someone to simply have a great day. But if you think about it, that includes everything. Hard to have a great day if you're sick or in dire need. So, to pray that someone would have a great day is to pray that all of their needs are met.

Takeaway: I hope you have a great day.

37

When a playwright gets a show produced it is nothing short of a miracle. So, you can imagine my delight when Aurora Theatre announced that my comedy *Greener Pastures* would be a part of their 2020 season. I was in seventh heaven. And then, well, Covid happened. The 2020 lockdown was hard for everyone. And as you probably know, all things theater/live performance also came to a screeching halt. I, along with many artists had productions, cancelled. The cancellation was especially distressing because I had been courting this theater since 2012. But what could I do? The world was shutdown. And then, Aurora did the most amazing thing. They informed me they would instead be streaming a production of my musical *Barbara's Blue Kitchen* in their 2020 season. (https://www.concordtheatricals.com/p/4994/barbaras-blue-kitchen) The BBK production was beautiful and I will be forever grateful that Ann-Carol Pence produced *Barbara's Blue Kitchen* during that tumultuous time.

I still, however, had a hope that Aurora would circle back to *Greener Pastures* at some point. So, I tried to stay gently in the mix by occasionally calling and sending updated drafts. That's why, In the fall of 2022, I decided to produce a reading of my newest *Greener Pastures* draft in New York City. I cast an amazing group of actors, brought on a director, booked a space and flew to NYC for a reading of my play. I was so excited to hear this newest version out loud. We rehearsed for a few hours after which, an audience filed into the room and we performed the play. The reading went exceedingly well and the feedback afterwards was extremely positive. And on a good news note, after hearing about the reading, Aurora Theatre asked that I send them the newest draft. They read the new draft and then, to my happy surprise, committed to producing the show in their 2024 season. And let me just say, their 2024 season announcement was a dream-come-true coming true. **Takeaway: We often, especially in the arts community, wait for someone else to come and rescue us, someone who will show up and produce our work, but sometimes, we simply have to put one foot in front of the other and rescue ourselves. What activity would bring you joy today? What subject or activity do you want to know more about?**

38

Remember that not so great neurologist that I mentioned? Well, after asking, literally, every doctor we went to if they had any neurologist recommendations. Mom's new geriatric doctor recommended Dr. Brett Parker, who happens to be an overall wonderful neurologist. He listens intently to mom whenever we visit and gives excellent care. You gotta love a doctor that looks your loved one in the eye, asks them questions and pays attention to what your loved one has to say. **Takeaway: Find doctors who look your loved ones in the eyes. Doctors who ask them questions and then, listen to their answers.**

39

As I've mentioned, traveling can be stressful, but traveling with senior citizens can be doubly stressful, but when your niece is getting married, travel you must. As I've mentioned, we're a musical family. Our dad is a songwriter. My cousin is a songwriter, I'm a songwriter. My brother is a songwriter and mom continually surrounded by music, well, she has been pulled into numerous co-writes as well. What can I say? Music is the "go-to" in our family. So, before traveling, we (dad, mom, Cousin Richard and I) wrote and recorded the wedding song *What a Day*. Then, we packed ourselves into the car and set off for the celebration. The drive was a joy fest, but sitting for that long can be difficult for seniors. So, we often stopped to stretch and take short walks. Side note: Richard drove us to my older niece's wedding in years prior. And yes, we wrote a song for those nuptials as well. We will be forever grateful to Richard for making both wedding trips and for the many other kindnesses he has shown over the years. He and his wife Liz are (in our collective opinion) two of the finest humans on the planet. **Takeaway: Regularly stopping for short walks on long drives is a must for the elderly.**

40

In the fall of 2022, dad met with a cataract surgeon re: cataract surgery. We picked up the prescribed eye drops, set the date and on the appointed day, off we went to get dad's first eye done. Mom and I waited, prayerful, in the waiting room. And after a while, they informed us that the patient was ready to be picked up. Then, they wheeled dad out to the car and said the **WORDS WE DID NOT WANT TO HEAR. "There's been a complication. Part of the cataract has fallen to the back of your father's eye and to remove the cataract piece will require an additional surgery."** Wait, what? Later, dad recounted that the doctor had said an ominous, "Ooooh, I've never seen that before" during the procedure causing a chill of terror to run through him. Did I mention that the date was November 22nd? Two days before Thanksgiving? Did I mention that there's a 1% chance of this calamity happening? We took dad home, trying not to give in to total anxiety re: whether this might affect dad's vision longterm.

The phrase "**the squeaky wheel gets the grease**" is a saying for a reason. So, I kept squeaking and called the
105

cataract surgeon's office literally every hour. I was determined to somehow get dad set up with a retina specialist before the holiday weekend. I was pleasant, but firm. Finally, the cataract surgeon called me back to set up an appointment for dad to meet with him the next morning. So, early the next day, we trudged over to the cataract surgeon's office. He checked out dad's eye and promptly sent us an elevator ride up to a retina specialist. Did I mention that dad was surgery ready? Yes, even though we hadn't even met with the retina specialist yet. Yes, the surgery had not been scheduled. But, nonetheless, **we arrived ready for surgery. You're not supposed to consume food or fluids before surgery. With that in mind, I had told dad to not eat or drink anything that morning. "Only drink a sip of water when taking your pills." I told him. So, when we met with the retina specialist, I told the good doctor, "In case there's room on your schedule this afternoon, my dad has not consumed any fluids or food." "Is this true?" He asked my father. "Yes." Dad informed him. And with that, dad was put onto the afternoon schedule.**

As I drove dad to the hospital, if you can believe it, the low tire light came on in the car. (Yowza!) I dropped dad off, got him situated, drove home, switched cars, and raced back to the hospital with mom. (It was later discovered that the tire had a nail in it.) The whole ordeal was stressful. All I could do the whole time was pray. I mainly prayed for the surgeon's steady skillful hands and that dad would not end up blind in his eye.

Thankfully, the operation went off without a hitch. And yippee-kay-yay, dad's eye healed and, other than, the part where the cataract piece fell to the back of his eye, the cataract surgery had been successful as well. The next day, even though it was Thanksgiving, the retina specialist kindly examined dad's eye post-op. And told dad everything looked great and that the cataract piece was definitely gone. I was now, once again, on eye drop duty. Also, since dad couldn't drive as his eye healed, I had to cart him around town for the next month. Dad's main daily destination was to see his friend Robert Lewis. Dad had been having morning meetings with his friend Robert for years. Both music business aficionados, they would sit around drinking coffee and talking about songs, songwriting, songwriters and country music. Rather than go back home during these visits, mom and I decided to drop dad off and go on our own adventures. Mom has always been one of my favorite companions. So, this worked out perfectly. We'd pop into various places for coffee or a treat of some sort and have some delicious fun. (Sadly in 2023, Robert fell backwards down a flight of stairs and, after healing, moved away to Hawaii to be near his family, which was a gain for his kids, but a definite loss for dad. Life sure does take unwieldy twists and turns.)

As dad's eye healed and time passed, dad developed amazing vision in the post-op eye. He was, understandably, unwilling to have the second eye done though. So, his vision, without glasses, is a bit lopsided. Maybe down the road, he'll change his mind, but after such a harrowing experience, that's for him to decide.

Not long after dad's eye fiasco, dad had another appointment with his cardiologist who recommended that dad take a treadmill nuclear stress test. The nurse who was present looked a lot like Jesus. To clarify, he resembled various paintings that depicted Jesus. And when dad first saw him, he thought that Jesus was in the room. And dad was like, "Uh-oh, what's going on here?" Then, the guy approached to escort dad into the stress test room. Once dad realized he wasn't having a vision/dying, he was cracking jokes throughout the whole procedure. Needless to say, the stress test went well.

We also had car trouble (again) around this time. So, looking back, this was a pretty full tilt season. But the car got fixed and the stress test showed that dad's heart was doing just fine.

Takeaway: Don't be afraid to be a squeaky wheel on behalf of your loved one or yourself.

41

....

This time it was mom's rheumatologist that prescribed PT at Results Physiotherapy where she did both Physical and Occupational Therapy. Dad would take her and while he waited, he would sit in a nearby chair working on his memoir, *The Writing on the Wall,* which I later self-published for him through *Book Baby.*

Ironically, on one of mom's visits, dad was hurrying towards the entrance and fell down on the hard concrete. This then, caused the arthritis in his back to flair up again, which led to a doctor visit where dad was also prescribed physical therapy also at Results Physiotherapy. Both parents got noticeably stronger and better. So, thanks Results PT for the good results. **Takeaway: Maybe don't hurry so much?**

Kathy

42

....

In February, 2023, I found out that my cousin Kathy was in hospice. There are things during my lifetime that I wish I had done. For example, my friend Suzanne asked me to sing at her dad's memorial and because of lack of money, I said I couldn't. If I could do that moment over, I would choose to show up. But what can I say? Hindsight's twenty-twenty and I just didn't see things the way that I see them now. People are more important. Connection with those who are dear to us is important and if there's a way to show up for your friends and family, show up. Scrounge the money together and show up. I'm not saying don't have healthy boundaries. I'm not saying don't take care of yourself. I'm simply saying do whatever will cause deeper connections.

All this said, when I found out that my cousin who was way too young to be in hospice was in hospice, I made plans and I booked a flight because I had every intention of going to see her before she passed. But on the day I was supposed to fly out, dad's back acted up. I took him for x-rays. Thankfully nothing was broken, but still I had to postpone my flight.

Not long after, however, I was scheduled to fly to NYC for a pre-birthday trip. I had even booked a space to perform along with other artists. I had bought tickets to a few broadway shows and scheduled time with friends. Dad's back was much improved by then, but to be on the safe side, **I hired a caregiver for the dates I would be gone. I needed to know that, in case dad's back acted up again, there would be someone who could and would help them. I also cooked all of mom and dad's meals. This way, there would be no cooking/turning on the stove while I was away. All they had to do was to pop the meals into the microwave and eat.** Everything went off without a hitch. Dad's back was back to normal, mom's needs were met and the caretaker was caring. She was not, however, a country music fan, nor was she all that interested in dad's jokes. So, it wasn't as fun perhaps as they would have hoped. But she was there, helping and no bad things happened while I was away. I'll take it as a win.

A month later, when I, once again, prepared to go and see my cousin Kathy, dad wasn't too keen on my bringing the caregiver back. Instead, I gave dad her number, asking him to call the caregiver if his back pain returned and off I went. Seeing Kathy was a highpoint. Even though her health was unstable, I helped her decorate the walls in her room. I thought seeing photos of family would brighten her remaining days. Cousin Richard, Kathy's brother, was there

111

as well and the three of us went out for barbecue, Kathy's favorite meal. Several months after I visited, Kathy passed away. Needless to say, I was super glad that I'd gotten to see her. She was so loving and supportive to me as a child. She was a good deal older than me, but she always treated me with respect and made me feel like a somebody. She was a kind soul with a contagious laugh. She had an amazing singing voice and I loved her very, very much. **Takeaway: If someone you love is in hospice, now is the time to go and see them.**

The Importance of Family Trips

43

In the spring of 2023, Cousin Richard, once again, picked mom, dad and I up for yet another adventure. This time no songwriting occurred, but still, a lot of fun. We met up with family members for a bonafide family vacation in the mountains. The trip was a birthday gift from my brother Robbi and sister-in-law Janet, but the real gift was mom and dad being seen and getting to see everyone. (I, of course, brought the wedge pillow once again with the hope that mom's sleep would be sound, which it was.) On one night, the whole family sat around singing. What a great and harmonious time. As I sit here remembering it, I am struck by the kind generosity of my brother and sister-in-law. They really have gone out of their way to make beautiful family vacations over the years. And, as a caregiver, these breaks have been phenomenally beneficial. **Takeaway: Make trips to see family as often as possible. If your family is gone or too toxic for you to do this, make trips to see friends as often as possible. My point is, find ways to connect with the people who support and love you. Our connections are so important. No family or friend is perfect, but I recommend showing up for one another, love as hard as you can and when things don't go exactly right, keep trying. In other words, don't give up on one another.**

Producing My Play Petie

44

....

As I've mentioned, I'm ever interested in creative outlets. That said, I got it into my head to co-produce my play *Petie* at the Darkhorse Theater in Nashville. I've gotten to perform in this play in Charlotte, NC, New York City and at the Women's Theatre Festival. These characters, this world had been in my heart for years. In fact, figuring out how to write this play was the main reason I applied to/went to grad school. I was determined to figure out how to turn the short story that I'd written, titled *Petie*, into a play. To this day, the play is one of my favorite creations. However, I had never performed the show in Nashville. So, I set my mind to making a Nashville production happen. I teamed up with my ever-talented friends Lauren and Kenny, two fellow artist/producers, and we began putting all the production pieces together. If you want to bring a project to life, team up with fellow "doers." A lot of people talk about doing projects, but to take it past the talking stage, you have to find likeminded people who are willing to turn the dream into a reality. The three of us agreed that we would act in and co-produce the show and that's what we did. We put our resources together, held auditions, rehearsed, created/built the set and ultimately, performed the play together. The cast was terrific, the show was well-attended and Bonnie, the role that I portrayed was, once again, a joy to perform.

Beautiful friends and glorious neighbors toted mom and dad back and forth to the theater, enabling them to literally attend every show. (Dad and mom had even run lines with me as I prepared.) **For my entire life mom and dad have been so steadfastly loving. Their encouragement of**

me/my writing/acting is one of the reasons taking care of them is, for the most part, actually enjoyable. Love streams through and out of them effortlessly. Numerous cousins also attended the play, some even journeyed all the way from Iowa. (Thanks Patty, Sandy, Susan and Pam!) It was a fabulous and wonderful time. Getting to perform *Petie* in Nashville and getting to see all of the people who attended filled my creative cup, which made me quite happy and as a by-product, made me a more joyful caregiver. Again, if you're a writer, consider booking a space and presenting your work. If you're a dancer, bond with fellow dancers, book a space and dance. If you want to learn how to play pickle ball, find a partner and play. If you want to crochet or knit, start a crochet or knitting circle. There is no better time than now to start. And if one passion project doesn't work for you, look into trying another. **Takeaway: Team up with fellow "doers" and bring your dreams to life.**

45

··

After years of avoiding it, the three of us came down with Covid. Dad had a low grade fever. Mom had the sniffles. I had a scratchy throat. So, just to be safe, I took us all to a Vanderbilt walk-in clinic and to our surprise, we all tested positive. I took Paxlovid and mom and dad took Molnupiravir. Thankfully, all we felt was tired. We slept solid for five days. We slept and slept and then, thankfully, we were better.

Not long after my bout with Covid, I, at long last, finished painting the outside of the house. (I had been painting it as weather permitted for many months.) I'd listen to a podcast or an audible book and paint. And little by little, the entire house got done. In fact, I finished it on the day that my great niece was born. I wanted to be doing something important when she made her arrival and I figured painting a house fit the bill. **Takeaway: The key re: house painting, in my opinion, is to buy very expensive paint. This way, you'll only have to apply one coat. I also recommend that you hire a handyman or woman to paint the high parts.**

116

46

After four years of caregiving, I gave myself a big vacation. I am half Irish and going to Ireland had been on my bucket list for years. And so I, along with my longtime friend Laura, decided to take the plunge. To say that I felt at home there is putting it lightly. I absolutely loved Ireland. The grass is so green. No wonder it's called the Emerald Isle. The food, the beer. I'm not a huge drinker, but I do enjoy dark beers and to be in the land of Guinness… delicious. Beamish, another dark beer, also quite tasty. The main thing was to take a breather, soak up the beautiful sites and simply relax. It was glorious to not be needed for a wee bit. I am a fan of service, but even the server sometimes needs a break. After touring Dublin, we took a train to Cork to stay with my dear friend Roger Ryan. From Cork we took a day trip to the Cliffs of Moher, a day trip to see the Ring of Kerry and on another day Roger toted us to Tipperary where I got to sit in the very church that my ancestors would have attended. Precious, precious time.

As you know from an earlier story, my family didn't take vacations to faraway places. So, going to a place like Ireland was a big move for me financially. However, I didn't go into debt doing it. I carefully saved up for the trip. I also saved a boatload of money on housing by staying with friends. The upshot was, I was able to eat great food and see all the splendid Irish sites while staying within my budget. I mention this with the hope of encouraging you to treat yourself to a big break. Google "cheap, delicious eats" in your destination city or eat a few simple meals of an orange and a bag of cashews or some amazing fish and chips from Leo Burdock's in Dublin.

Update re: my parents: while I was gone, my brother hosted my parents for a few days at his house. And for the days mom and dad were alone, I'd lined up various friends and neighbors to stop in and say hi. Plus, as always, I'd cooked meals and planned lunches for every day/night that I'd be away. I'd also laid out two weeks worth of pills for mom. (Dad does his own pills.) And I, of course, called daily, just to make sure that all was well. **Takeaway: Yes, traveling to faraway places can be expensive, but I recommend finding ways to financially make it work. Get discounted tickets, buy a simple lunch of an orange and a bag of cashews, fish and chips or a sandwich. Or Google "cheap eats" in the cities you're visiting. Use public transportation. The bottom line is, you deserve a break. Studies show that caregivers have a 63% higher mortality rate than non-caregivers. Let's face it, there is a physical, emotional, spiritual toll to caregiving. It's a very stressful job. We simply must take time to recuperate. So, if you're a caregiver, give yourself the**

gift of travel. Even if it's just two towns over relaxing at an AirBNB for a few days, give yourself a loving break.

Urology, Neuropathy & Podiatry

47

In September 2023, dad went to see a urologist. He was then scheduled for a cystoscopy, which would allow his urologist to see the lining of his bladder. Thankfully, everything looked normal and there were no complications. The things people have to go through! Dad was also feeling a great deal of foot pain because of, yet another, ingrown toenail during this time. So, he met with a podiatrist who removed the ingrown toenail. **After the aforementioned ingrown toenail episode, dad and mom are now seeing their podiatrist every three months to get their toenails clipped.**

Dad also suffers regularly from neuropathy for which he's tried numerous solutions. He's tried soaking his feet in Epsom Salts, soaking his feet in water, putting Vick's Vapor Rub on his feet, putting a specially made medicinal cream on his feet. One night, I even put arnica (anti-inflammatory) cream onto dad's feet, which did provide a bit of relief. **Wanting to get more blood flow to the bottom of his feet, dad also regularly massages his feet on a foot massager.** Recently, after consulting Google once again, **I soaked dad's feet in warm turmeric, cayenne, rosemary, salt water and (thankfully) dad slept soundly through the night. If you use this method, be sure to have a towel ready for afterwards so that your carpet doesn't turn yellow from the turmeric.** All of the above methods alleviated dad's neuropathy to varying degrees, but none of the above have solved or eradicated the issue.

Continuing on the foot theme, both of my parents have struggled with **toe fungus. Here are two products that I highly recommend: FungaBlend 10 Tolnaftate Anti-fungal Solution (can be ordered online) and the other one is Ciclopirox Gel 0.77%, which needs a prescription.** If your loved one is battling foot fungus, I suggest that you ask their physician about the aforementioned products. **Takeaway: Set up a yearly appointment with a podiatrist to get your loved one's feet checked out. And, if possible, get them scheduled every three months for a toenail clipping sessions, since ingrown toenails can be quite painful.**

48

In October of 2023, I decided to do whatever it would take to get dad's memoir finished and self-published. So, I compiled all of his stories and, with the help of our friend Rick and cousins Corky and Susan, every last story got typed up and formatted. Each story pertained to a song that dad had written. I also typed up the lyrics to all of the songs that dad mentions in each story. Dad has written A LOT of songs, over two thousand to be exact. Although not all of his songs were included in the book, this was no small endeavor. After proofreading the manuscript, I contacted *Book Baby* and had copies of his book *The Writing on the Wall a songwriter's journey from Wilton, Iowa to Nashville, Tennessee* printed up. Truly one of the most soul satisfying projects I've been a part of. Dad was thrilled to hold his very own book in his hands. Then, at the end of December, we threw a book launch party for fifty people. Fellow songwriters got up and sang songs they'd co-written with dad. My brother and niece sang. I, backed up by our neighbors Pam and Steven, crooned a song or two as well. It was an unforgettable evening. The high point was seeing the look of sheer happiness on dad's face. Since then, he's been working on a second memoir that focuses on growing up poor, his life as a child, his mother, the death of his musician father and funny things that have happened to him as he journeyed and ultimately achieved a successful songwriting career. I am absolutely looking forward to putting that book together for him in the near future. (Get ready for round two, Corky and Susan!) **Takeaway: Does your loved one still have their mental faculties intact? If so, you might want to Google memoir writing programs to help your loved one get their story out and onto the page. There are numerous self-publishing avenues available: Book Baby, Apple Books, Amazon and Ingramspark, to name a few.**

Kindness Matters, a Short Film

49

I decided to put Dallas Boczulak, one of my screen acting students, into a short film. My hope was that this would help him create a reel, which might, down the road, garner him work. Plus, he'd hopefully see himself up on the big screen in a film festival. Making a film, even a short one is no small task, but I wanted to support this student's dream. He's a natural on film and the camera absolutely loves him. So, I asked Dallas if he wanted to perform a role in a short film. He said yes and so, I set the project into motion. First, I converted my ten-minute play *Right Matters* into a screenplay, changing one of the featured roles so that it more aptly fit the student. (I ultimately changed the title as well to *Kindness* Matters.) And to get things rolling, I cast Phil Vassar in the lead role. Phil, an amazing actor and singer, is also featured in my feature film *Chasing Taste,* a romantic comedy that was directed by Sean Gannet, which is available on Amazon Prime. (https://www.amazon.com/Chasing-Taste-Kirk-McGee/dp/B072NQLCGT) Phil also portrays the role of Warren in my short film *i only miss you when i'm breathing,* which was directed by Ashley Wren Collins. I cast longtime great actor and Lipscomb University Alum Michael Diallo McLendon as well. And, since I love to act, I cast myself in the role of Morgan. Then, I brought Meredith, one of my film students on board to produce. She, in turn, hired numerous Lipscomb University students for the crew. As you can imagine, making a film requires money. So, I launched a funding site. (Big thank you to fellow producers Gary & Jo Reamey, JBoz and all of the grass roots contributors that contributed along the way.) The brilliant Matt Huesmann agreed to be our cinematographer. And finally, my good buddy Dave DeBorde, stepped in to direct. It took two days to shoot. Then, our editor Jay Whittle, got busy editing and our composer Taylor Reed got busy composing the score. It was a glorious labor of love and I'm so proud of the work that was done and for each artist that was involved. I also had the great honor of co-writing the closing credits song, *Hug the World,* with my sweet dad and Phil Vassar.

Why in the world would I do all this? Well, first and foremost, I love to collaborate. But it also gave me something creative to focus on while continuing to love on/care for my parents. And so far, I'm happy to report that the screenplay was an Official Selection for the Austin Short Film Festival and that the produced short film was an Official Selection for the Sunscreen Film Festival (while it was titled *Right Matters)* and, under the title *Kindness Matters,* the film was an Official Selection for The Big Apple Film Festival, New Filmmakers Plus NY 2024 and 2025 online Film Festival and the Chicago Indie Film Awards. Attending the Big Apple Film Festival was a career highlight. Sitting in the sold out theater in NYC, surrounded by friends, hearing the audience laugh was a complete joy. Thanks for including our film BAFF! **Takeaway: If you want to make something, I hope some part of this story encourages you to take the leap and just do it.**

50

In December 2023, I took mom to a Vanderbilt Walk-in Clinic. She had a persistent cough that kept hanging on. So, I wanted to have her chest x-rayed to rule out pneumonia. The x-rays showed that her lungs were clear. So, the doctor prescribed benzonatate, also known as Tessalon Perles. This drug has a whole boatload of possible side effects, including confusion, hallucinations, seizures etc. Simultaneously, it can also relieve a cough and, as I mentioned, was doctor recommended. Mom tried it for two weeks, but her cough did not improve. In fact, her cough continued into the new year. So, on January 9th, 2024, I took her to see Dr. Stout where we learned that mom's pulse was jacked up to 144 and she had a low grade fever of 99.4. The doctor promptly ushered us out of her office and towards the nearby emergency room at Vanderbilt. Not the day we were expecting. We drove the two short blocks and entered a very crowded ER. Because the doctor was worried that mom had a pulmonary embolism, a life threatening blood clot in her lungs, we got into an ER room relatively quickly. They did the necessary tests, blood work and took a urine sample. And what they discovered was that mom did not have a pulmonary embolism. Instead she had a urinary tract infection, which had triggered **atrial fibrillation, an abnormal heart rhythm due to an inflammatory response in mom's body. Let me get this straight, mom had a urinary tract infection and that UTI had caused A-Fib and the main symptom was a cough?!** How could we have possibly known this? After a bit of a wait, mom was admitted, given a room in the hospital and slated to have a **Cardioversion. This is when they shock the heart back into correct rhythm.** The procedure has a ninety percent success rate. But it can also lead to death. Evidently, one in one thousand people die from it. So, it was stressful to say the least, but what could we do? We needed to get mom's heart rate back to normal. We also had to wait two and a half days for them to actually perform the procedure because the hospital was, as I mentioned, overcrowded. In the meantime, I spent basically every moment with mom, passing time during the day and sleeping on the recliner chair by her bedside at night. I did this because, as I mentioned earlier, I believe as a caregiver that it's best to be as present as possible. Especially since, hospitals can sometimes be understaffed. and, let's face it, humans make mistakes. This is not me bashing doctors or nurses. Our mom was a fantastic OB nurse before she retired. It's just that according to Johns Hopkins Medicine "250,000 deaths occur in American hospitals every year. Medical error is currently the third leading cause of death in the U.S." and, as I mentioned before, people who have advocates statistically receive better care. Dad was there all day every day as well. I just didn't think sleeping on a recliner was good for dad and his arthritic back. So, he didn't do the hospital sleepovers.

Before the Cardioversion, I told mom everything I wanted to say, just in case she was one of the one in one thousand. I called my brother so that he could do the same. Dad was, as you might remember, in the one percent re: his cataract surgery complications. So, I wasn't taking any chances. I was also doing a great deal of praying.

Hallelujah, she pulled through just fine. Well, not totally fine. **The shock of the Cardioversion, left a square burn mark on mom's back. For this, the nurses loaded me up with Petroleum Hydrating Ointment, Latex gloves, xeroform petroleum dressing, extra absorbent pads and first aid tape so that I could do burn care on her back once we were back at home.** Before leaving, we picked up mom's new prescription of Eliquis, which is a blood thinner. When a person goes into A-Fib their heart can throw out blood clots. Eliquis thins the blood. Thus, protecting the patient from possible strokes. Mom had been on Eliquis briefly after the hip break, but now, it looks like she's on it for good. Mom's Diltiazem, a blood pressure medication, was also increased from 120 mg to 180 mg. And then, we headed home. I don't really have words for those days at the hospital. All I know is, when you love someone there's never enough time with them and I was very grateful to get more time with mom. One of the things we began doing post hospital, was to simply **use**

disposable personal body wipes/pre-moistened wash cloths after every poo. Better safe than sorry. I'm not sure that, as the saying goes, "cleanliness is next to godliness," but I am sure that UTI's are caused by bacteria buildup so, the less bacteria the better. Also, **thanks to our other handyman Rick, we've installed a bidet.** My hope is the bidet will replace the need for the pre-moistened, disposable wash cloths since over time they can irritate the skin.

One quick note about boundaries. At one point, I took mom to her urology appointment post hospital stay. When the nurse took mom's blood pressure, her bp was a bit higher than normal. So, I asked him to take it again, but in the other arm. (Years ago, mom had a mastectomy on one side. Afterwards, the surgeon recommended that her blood pressure be taken on the non-operative side moving forward. This is typically what we have done since her mastectomy, but, on that particular morning, I hadn't noticed that he had taken it on the operative side of mom's body.) Long story short, the nurse refused. I asked again and he simply wouldn't retake mom's blood pressure and ended by saying, "It doesn't matter what her bp is since she is not here for that." Uh… it doesn't matter? Once the urologist came into room, I recounted the story and asked that that nurse never be mom's nurse again. Yes, people can have a bad day, but the behavior was unacceptable. Also, because mom had recently gone into atrial fibrillation, keeping track of her blood pressure is, now more than ever, important. The doctor sent a different nurse in for the next part of the exam. **To stave off future UTI's the urologist prescribed Estradiol Vaginal Cream USP 0.01% as well as probiotics and Cranberry pills with D-Mannose, which, according to Google and the doctor, stops bacteria from sticking to the urinary tract walls.** I highly recommend that you consult a medical professional re: preventative care if your loved one is repeatedly contracting urinary tract infections.

Being a caregiver can lead you into uncomfortable waters, but, if someone displays disregard for the patient, your loved one, it is, in my humble opinion, imperative that you find someone else to care for them. Over the course of these pages, there have been two uninvolved doctors (one female, one male) who we replaced and two nurses (one male, one female) and one radiographer that had angry bedside manners. I point this out to say, they are not the norm. Most of the nurses, doctors and medical practitioners we have had the honor to deal with have been stellar. Also, all of the doctors that I've praised in this book are in our experience praise worthy. That said, only you and your loved one know what physicians/medical professionals are the best fit for you/them.

Takeaway: Invest in a bidet.

51

After we returned home from the hospital, it snowed and then, it snowed some more. Our street was a solid sheet of ice. The hospital stint was behind us, but I, my body, didn't feel quite normal. So, a good friend, who has four wheel drive, braved the icy streets and carted me to a walk-in clinic. I took a test only to find out that I had picked up a bacteria. The nurse asked, "Have you been in the hospital?" "Yes, my mom was in the hospital and I stayed by her bedside for two and a half days. Why?" I asked. "Well, you've picked up Klebsiella, which is usually found in hospitals" the nurse responded. Let me get this straight, I helped out my mom, supported my mother and now, I've come down with an antibiotic resistant bacteria? Yes, folks, this can happen. **While supporting your loved one at the hospital, you might be exposed to something that harms you. So, sterilize your hands and sterilize the surfaces in your loved one's room.** Of course, hospitals have a cleaning staff. But, as I mentioned, the hospital was extremely busy during this time. All this said, I was now praying that the ciprofloxacin that I was on would kick the bacteria out of my system. Guess what? It didn't. After a week of Cipro, I had to go on Amoxicillin-Clav, which thankfully, did clear my body of the bacteria.

It's funny how things work out sometimes. I had had stomach problems since 2013. I'd tried all that I knew to try. I'm lactose intolerant. So, I'd given up dairy. I went on the Whole 30 diet numerous times. I regularly did intermittent fasting. I gave up processed (for the most part) foods. I limited alcohol consumption. No matter what I did, at the end of the night, my stomach was on fire. I had even ordered an at home H.pylori test. **Helicobacter pylori, is a bacteria that infects your stomach and is present in over half of the world. It causes, among other things, bloating and a burning in your stomach that is worse when your stomach is empty. H. pylori is also a common cause of peptic ulcers.** For some reason, I hadn't taken the home test that I had purchased yet. But here I was taking this antibiotic that supposedly upsets your stomach, but instead my stomach was feeling better than it had in years. I looked up both **Ciprofloxacin and Amoxicillin-Clav and learned that both of these antibiotics kill H. pylori.** Could it be that I'd stumbled into a cure? After I finished the Amoxicillin-Clav, the Klebsiella was gone. (Yay!) Still, my stomach didn't feel completely healed. It was, however, 80% better. So, I researched how **H. pylori is traditionally treated and discovered that antibiotics are usually given along with Olmezprazol (Prilosec.)** I bought some over the counter and then, put myself on three days of Olmezprazol. Side note: If you take this drug, watch out. "Long-term use can interfere with

131

Calcium absorption, which is crucial for bone health."
(according to Google) Olmezprazol also causes a bit of a
headache. So, I decided to give up caffeine at the same
time. I'd been researching the effects of coffee on the
stomach as well. I love coffee, but I began to wonder if my
daily two cups were exacerbating my stomach symptoms.
As I've previously mentioned, I'm not a doctor, nurse or
health professional. All I know is, what I've experienced.
And what I experienced after taking the antibiotics, going
on Olmezprazol for a limited time and giving up caffeine,
was relief. And ever since then, my stomach issues are
essentially gone. This was a huge "amen" moment because,
let's face it, it cannot be healthy to have prolonged
inflammation in the body. (On a side note, I have been able
to add a half cup of coffee a day back into my diet, but I no
longer drink coffee on an empty stomach.)

Speaking of inflammation… automotive inflammation,
that is. After the snow melted, I went to start the car and the
engine light came on. (Ugh!) Turns out, during the snow
storm, mice had moved into the engine and the little
critters had eaten the engine wires. Six hundred dollars
worth of new wires later, the car was fine. I also bought an
ultrasonic mouse repeller for under the hood of the car.
Just in case, they tried to come back. The mouse repeller
emits a sound that mice hate. So, find another home mice!

On an unrelated note, in 2023 my cholesterol had crept
up to 155. So, looking for answers I read the book *How Not
to Die* by Dr. Michael Greger. The book had a considerable
impact on my meat intake and I decided to become more

of a flexitarian. Meaning, I eat less meat and more lentils, fruits, vegetables and beans, which I love. After a year of eating a primarily plant based diet, my cholesterol was back down to 128.

Takeaway: If my stomach problems sound familiar, I suggest you get tested by a medical professional for H. pylori.

Swallowing Problems

52

If dad doesn't chew his food enough, it causes him discomfort/esophageal dysphagia, a sensation that the food is stuck in his chest. He literally has to stop eating and wait for the feeling to pass. The feeling became so jarring, I booked dad for a swallow test to find out more information. Sadly, not much came of the swallow test because I had inadvertently double booked appointments. So, I was not available for that particular appointment since I was at another appointment with mom. Anyway, because I wasn't present, the pertinent information got lost in translation. This is why **it's good to have an advocate go**

with your loved ones to doctor appointments. Let's face it, going to the doctor can be stressful and retaining all that gets said can be difficult. Best to have someone who will take notes on the patient's behalf, someone who can manage all of the online sign-ins, doctor reports and in-office comments is a plus. Even though not much came of dad's appointment, I used that experience to request that he chew his food more, which he now does. **Chewing our food 32 times is SO IMPORTANT.** Whenever dad remembers to chew 32 times, he's fine.

Dad also went through a period where, in the middle of the night, he felt like he couldn't take a deep breath. He had pulmonary tests done and it was suggested that he use an inhaler, which dad opted not to do. And, over time, the "not being able to take a deep breath" sensation resolved itself on its own. **Takeaway: Experts say that chewing our food 32 times is important to our overall health.**

53

In November of 2023, Aurora Theatre flew me to Georgia to attend the auditions for their upcoming production of my comedy *Greener Pastures*. It was so great to be there and quite fabulous to sit in on the auditions/get to know the director. Then, in February 2024, the theater flew me back to sit in during the first week of rehearsals, during which they encouraged me to make any script changes that I thought necessary. The cast was a hoot and it was an absolute gift to be there. I was especially blessed to bond with V.J., the actress portraying Alberta. She, along with the rest of the cast, took the play to the next level of hilarity and words cannot express how awesome it was to watch this consummate group of artists (both cast and crew) as they rehearsed my play. On a side note, in the Atlanta airport security line my computer got picked up by another commuter and I accidentally picked up their computer. What a heart sinking moment that was when I opened the computer only to see a stranger's homepage. The man had a unique name though. So, I went on my iPhone's Facebook page, found someone with that name and left a message, "Do you have my computer? I have yours." Two weeks later, he messaged me back and we both sent off the wrong computers to their rightful owners. And in a few days, received our correct computers in return. Good story twist in what could have been a total drag.

In March, Aurora Theatre flew me back yet again for our *Greener Pastures* opening night. What an amazing production! So fun to hear the audience laughing. So, satisfying to see this version, this rewrite of the script being brought to life on-stage. Big-time thank you to Ann-Carol Pence, the Co-Founder/Producing Artistic Director, who is an absolute gem of a human, and to the aforementioned cast and crew. The production was even recommended by the Suzi Awards. Thank you, Suzi Awards! And one of the actors was nominated for a Suzi Award for his performance in the show.

A little back story… By the time the Aurora production occurred, I had been working on *Greener Pastures* since 2007, not continually, but consistently. It had received its first production at The Cumberland County Playhouse, also a lovely production in 2017 with a stellar cast, crew and director. True to playwright form, as soon as I got back home from Aurora Theatre, I tweaked the script yet again. Writing is rewriting as they say and "they" are right.

Each time I left town to head off to Georgia, I, once again, planned lunches and cooked and froze every supper for my parents, labeling each one as well as, booking friends and neighbors to drop in/lay eyes on them/make sure they were okay. From my parent's side, they missed me when I was gone, but they are, as I've mentioned, extremely supportive of my writing and were happy that one of my dreams was coming to fruition. **Takeaway: Long awaited dreams can and do come true.**

Urinary Tract Infection & Three Rounds of Antibiotics

54

In March, dad was diagnosed with another UTI. This one proved quite difficult to get rid of. In fact, he had to go through three rounds of antibiotics. Dad was ultimately diagnosed with cystitis. This is a type of UTI that causes inflammation of the bladder. Evidently, changes in a man's prostate gland can leave elderly men more susceptible to urinary tract infections and, strangely, constipation can cause them as well. To keep constipation at bay, as I mentioned earlier, **have your loved one drink a bit of prune juice every morning. Also, as previously mentioned, have them take a Cranberry with D-Mannose tablet every day and a probiotic once or twice a week.** Dad (and mom's) urologist prescribed this for them and they've been doing well ever since. While we're on the topic of things that might be helpful, throw in a **turmeric tablet, which helps arthritis, is anti-inflammatory and neuroprotective** a few times a week as well.

While I'm writing about strange conditions that suddenly pop up, I might as well mention that, at one point, dad developed **oral thrush** (candidiasis), which causes white lesions on the tongue. If left untreated, this condition can make it difficult over time for your loved one to swallow and speak. So, my amazing dentist, Dr. Spalding Green, prescribed dad an **anti-fungal oral rinse** which cleared the thrush right up. **Takeaway: Cranberry with D-Mannose, probiotics and turmeric are essential for my parents. If your loved one is struggling in some of these same areas, I suggest that you ask their doctor or urologist if any of these products might be of help.**

55

In May 2024, I booked a self-care get-away and traveled to see my amazing friend Dana and her family. To be honest, just seeing my friend was gift enough. Being in the presence of longtime friends, friends who have known you through the years is a salve to the soul and I returned to caregiving rejuvenated.

It's a good thing I felt rejuvenated too because, one day after returning, I carted mom and dad off to the airport and to the Midwest for an epic family trip. I had booked dad aisle seats with lots of legroom because he had developed airplane claustrophobia, but he really wanted to go on this trip. So, he overcame his anxiety and off we flew. We stayed in a fabulous airBNB. My dear brother flew in as well, and rented us a car. Once there, we were joined by the previously mentioned superstar cousin Richard. Why all of this hullabaloo? Good question. The main reason we were there was to celebrate dad's memoir. The Wilton Library (where his sister had once worked) was throwing dad a book dedication ceremony. After which they placed dad's book on a special hometown history/luminaries book shelf. Also, our wonderful cousins (dad's nieces) Debbie, Susan,

Sandy, Patty and Pam hosted a delicious lunch for us. During the lunch, dad got to see and hug his older sister Lois who is now 95. And the **Candy Kitchen, a turn of the century soda fountain that opened in 1910, threw dad a book party.** So many cherished cousins, relatives and old friends attended. Dad was in 7th heaven. Seeing family, driving past places that were meaningful to our parents, taking a tour of the houses where we once lived was a wonderful experience. And each night, after having driven to Davenport, Campbell's Island, Silvas etc., we sat around in our AirBNB playing cards. Every second of togetherness was a gift because, prior to that trip, mom and dad thought they'd never see these people or these old stomping grounds again. And yet, here they were. It felt sacred to be there and I'm so glad it all came together. So grateful for every person that showed up to see them.

   Takeaway: If you are a full-time caregiver, what place would inspire you or what activities will provide you with deep rest? Also, re: the person or people you're giving care to, what places or people might they want to see? How might you make your (and their) dreams come true?

56

As a result of mom's curved spine and the weakened skin from the Cardioversion burn, mom began to develop **pressure ulcers** on her back. Apart from **applying Petroleum hydrating ointment to the pressure ulcer, which keeps the bandage from sticking to the wound as it heals, the best wound dressing I've found is Neo G Opti-Heal Advanced Wound care Silicone Foam Absorbent Dressing.** This is an amazing product, expensive, but it absolutely works for/helps my mom.

At another point, mom was experiencing an urgency to "go" and great deal of discomfort when trying to do so. The problem was a fecal impaction. **A fecal impaction is when there is poo, but it won't come out.** According to Google, **people with Parkinson's are prone to this condition. Parkinson's has a neurological impact on the internal anal sphincter muscles, which, in turn, slows down bowel movement.** What to do?! How to help my dear mom out of this situation? What worked for us was a suppository. Also, I am now incorporating more fiber into mom's diet. **Takeaway: I highly recommend Neo G Opti-Heal Advanced Wound care Silicone Foam Absorbent**

Dressing for pressure ulcers and, when needed, stool softeners to keep things moving and grooving.

On the Brink of Promise

57

As I've mentioned, artists often find themselves waiting for someone else to swoop in and save the day. Oftentimes, that type of saving, simply doesn't take place. What if the person you're waiting for is you? What if you make the choice to move forward with or without outside help? Success in our society is defined by huge financial dividends. This one-dimensional definition can really mess with our heads. Don't get me wrong, I'm not against huge financial success. I'm just saying, I don't think waiting around for someone else to solve our problems/complete our dreams is healthy. Also, success can take many shapes. Success is finishing a second, third and fourth draft. Success is hosting a play reading in your living room. Success is submitting your play or screenplay to a theater or film festival. Success is getting Honorable Mention, or Semi-Finalist or Finalist. Success is putting the funds together and making a film in your backyard. Success is writing, dancing, painting no matter what. Writers need to write. Dancers need to dance. Painters need to paint. And quilters need to quilt. I also believe that work, oftentimes, begets work. If I hadn't continued doing rewrites on *Greener Pastures,* if I hadn't put together a reading of the play in NYC, Aurora Theatre wouldn't have read the draft that came as a result of the rewrites and the reading.

All this said, in August of 2024, I decided to take my own destiny into my own hands and produce and act in my play *On the Brink of Promise.* This play, which was commissioned by Theatre C, has had a good amount of encouragement along the way. It was given Special Consideration for the 2018 Relentless Award, included in Culture Project's Women Center Stage reading series as well as their Summer Reading Series. The play was a semi-Finalist for Unicorn Theatre's In-Progress Play Reading Series and a Semi-Finalist for the Eugene O'Neill Theater Center's National Playwrights Conference. Still, I had never seen it on stage. That said, I launched a funding site with my co-producers Bowen and Victoria, found a fabulous director, Kate Pierson, hired a phenomenal cast of actors, booked a rehearsal space, booked the Darkhorse Theatre and plunged into memorizing lines and on a, very low budget, put on four high class performances. Plus, I rewrote the play throughout the process and ended up with a much better version of the script by opening night.

(I've been working on this play, which was previously titled *The Displaced* and, at one point, *Land Grab* since 2009. So, having the play performed in front of an audience was a delight.) True to form, Mom and dad, brought to and fro by our wonderful neighbors and friends, attended all, but one performance. So fun to share the world of this play with them. I don't know if a theater will ever do a big time, full-fledged production of the piece, but, if they don't, at least I got to perform in it during this spectacular span of time. And because of the many script tweaks that I did on the script, the play was recently named as a Local Lab 14 semi-finalist! **Takeaway: Life is short. So, don't wait for someone else to make your dreams come true. Ban together with likeminded people and turn your dreams into realities.**

Atrial Fibrillation, Arthritic Knees & Physical Therapy

58

. . . .

I took mom and dad to see Dr. Rankin, their heart doctor. Both were doing well, except mom's heart was showing signs of atrial fibrillation again. The doctor didn't, however, think that she should have another Cardioversion, since her heart was most likely popping in and out of A-Fib at times. This was discouraging news. Mom, however, seemed and seems fine. So, that part is encouraging.

Not long after, going to see the cardiologist, dad fell down in the bathtub. No broken bones, but suddenly he had extreme knee pain. I took dad to see an orthopedic doctor for his knees. Dad's knees were x-rayed and showed signs of arthritis. I guess the jolt from the fall had set the knee pain into motion. So, they gave dad a steroid shot in both knees and referred dad to Star Physical Therapy. The thing about PT is it gets your loved one moving and grooving. And yes, they're not training him to run a marathon, but they are teaching him exercises that, hopefully, he'll now continue to do. And on a good news note, dad's knees have been markedly better since the steroid shots. Still, arthritis, joint inflammation, is a degenerative disease. So, he recently received gel shots in both knees as well.

One last caregiving tip: Mom's hands are always cold. This can affect the reading of the pulse oximeter. The pulse oximeter is the thing they put on your finger to check your pulse and oxygen during doctor visits. So, because mom's hands are regularly cold, I always hold her finger for five minutes before they put the oximeter on. This warms up her finger, which vastly helps the reading. I also remind mom to take deep breaths once her oxygen is being checked. **Takeaway: If your loved one's hands are cold, warm up their finger before getting their pulse/oxygen**

checked. Also, as we age, things beyond our control begin to happen in our bodies. In the face of this, eat well, sleep long, exercise and migrate towards gratitude at every turn.

Big Apple Film Festival and Beyond

59

. . . .

Regarding what's next on the caregiving front, I have no idea. "Open hands, open heart" is my motto as I love on my favorite two senior citizens. I've also, of late, been taking them to see old friends. Dad had been trying to get a hold of his longtime songwriting buddy Austin. So, a few months ago, I plugged Austin's assisted living address into my phone, piled us all into the car and headed off to Franklin, Tennessee. When we laid eyes on Austin, he was completely changed. So much so, we didn't recognize him at first. However, even though Austin had dementia and Parkinson's his eyes lit up when he saw dad. We sat down and played music from an album that dad, Austin and Charlie Black had in years past, written together. In between songs, dad told Austin stories about how they came up with the song ideas etc. and Austin's face beamed. A mere two weeks later, Austin passed away. And a week after hearing of Austin's passing, dad learned that his good buddy Robert had also passed on. Through tears, dad expressed how very glad he was that he got to see his longtime buddy Austin. Three weeks later, I took mom (and dad) to see mom's friend Pauline who has dementia. Happily, she recognized us and we sat around a table singing songs. Pauline and mom were nurses at the same hospital and had regularly met for lunch and gone to see many a movie together. As we drove away, mom said it was sad, but, like dad, she was glad that she'd gotten to see her wonderful friend Pauline. I also took dad and mom to see our dear friends Pippy and Freddy Weller. What a joy it was to spend time in their presence.

Every moment, every single moment is so precious with these two extraordinary human beings that I have the good fortune of calling mom and dad. This book is ending, but our journey together continues. I have no idea what's around the next bend, but I pray I'll handle it with wisdom, kindness and grace. **Takeaway: If there's someone you've been meaning to see, don't waste time. Make the time and just go.**

Hug the World

60

Thanks for reading my book! If you are a caregiver, I hope you found this book helpful. I also hope that you will take time to care for yourself while you care for others. And I want to encourage you to make time to follow your passion projects, even as you pick up prescriptions and make doctor's appointments, make time to do the things that bring you joy. And if you are a writer, write. In closing, I've decided to include the lyrics from the song that dad, Phil Vassar and I wrote for my short film *Kindness Matters*.

Hug the World
By Bobby Fischer, Lori Fischer & Phil Vassar

I came back again this morning.
It's so good to see your face.
My mind leaves me without warning.
I guess, that's the way it is these days.

Right now is picture perfect.
Everything's so crystal clear.
Every moment is a miracle.

I'm just happy to be here.

If I could hug the world,
heal the pain and all the hurt.
Fill it up with love, love, love.
I would, if I could, hug the world.

Who knows where I'll be tomorrow.
It's just too soon to know.
If I forget, please remember,
with all my heart I love you so.

If I could hug the world,
heal the pain and all the hurt.
Fill it up with love, love, love.
I would, if I could, hug the world.

Let me not forget to be faithful,
grateful, thankful.

If I could hug the world,
heal the pain and all the hurt.
Fill it up with love, love, love.
I would, if I could, hug the world.